Our Flower Girl

A Story of Grief
& Healing

Marilyn Fanning

Our Flower Girl: A Story of Grief & Healing
by
Marilyn Fanning

© 2003

Library of Congress Catalog Card Number: 2003109834
ISBN: 1890306487

Warwick House Publishing
720 Court Street
Lynchburg, VA 24504

DEDICATION

This book is dedicated to my grandsons,
Jason and Christopher Kennedy,
who have lived through a different kind of grief.

2 Cor 1:3, 4
Marilyn Fanning

ACKNOWLEDGMENTS

Without the help and encouragement of Regina Carson, Elaine Durand, George Everson, Marilyn Mateer, and Nancy Zappulla, this book would be unfinished pages stuffed in a drawer. Thank you, writers and friends!

TABLE OF CONTENTS

PREFACE

The doorbell rang for the fourth time. This time I gave the bread dough a good, hard punch. What now? First she wanted Kool-Aid. Then she needed to use the potty. Five minutes later her big sister took her doll and ran away. And now she was ringing the front door bell again!

Angrily, I grabbed the brass knob and flung open the door, yelling, even before I saw her. "Can't you stop ringing this bell? I'm BUSY!"

Small, sweaty hands extended a blob of purple to me. My eyes and heart focused on the offering of love. "These are for you, Mommy. For being a good mommy."

Claire, my five-year-old, handed me a bouquet of wilted violets, stems askew, blossoms crushed into a tight wad.

Wiping flour from my hands, I pulled the little girl onto my lap and sat in the hall chair. She pressed her head against me. "I love you, Mommy. I jus' needed a hug."

"I need a hug, too," I whispered. "A big one."

Forty years later our doorbell rang in a different house on a Sunday afternoon. This time there were two police officers at the door to tell us our daughter had died. The daughter with the violets.

Now there came other flowers, flowers of condolence. The kind of flowers I never wanted to have in my lifetime.

CHAPTER ONE

The Funeral

Claire, right, with sister Lesley

CHAPTER ONE

The Funeral

Our car moved slowly down the narrow gravel road, almost reluctantly, as if it absorbed the grief of its occupants. In the back seat sat our son Wayne, our daughter Lesley, and her husband Dick. Bill was at the wheel and I sat anxiously, hands on my lap. "Where are they? They should be here by now."

A slight pause in the back seat, "They'll be here, Mother."

"But we can't start without them!" I felt tears in my throat.

"They're coming. They'll be here."

Claire has two sons. Or is it HAD two sons? No, two sons, Jason and Christopher, once had a mother. They were coming with their father and their grandfather.

"They're behind us, Mother," Lesley reassured me.

As we approached the gravesite, I saw an expanse of grass, a casket under a canopy, and a tree that had overseen mourners many times, its leaves motionless as if in reverence.

We, the immediate family, were the last to arrive. Silently, people ringed the gravesite at a respectful distance. It seemed like a scene from a movie, not our daughter's death, not her funeral, but a video clip, the mourners were the actors. I felt like one of them. My job would be finished soon.

We joined the other relatives, the grandchildren, mostly grown, and people from out of town. But then I saw the group of people who had loved her deeply but differently. Some sat in wheelchairs, with others behind them grasping the handles. Heads were bent or thrust forward unnaturally. One had a leg missing. Several had Down syndrome. A brown-haired girl pressed a hanky to her eyes, both hands tight against her face.

As a program manager at Lynchburg Sheltered Industries, Claire's special gift was guiding these, her loved ones—those with mental and physical handicaps.

Now I was being seated in the front row before my daughter's casket. From some cavernous place, soundless cries pressed against my heart. I felt Jason's hand holding mine tightly. They weren't young children—they were nineteen and twenty-one, these boys. It had been Chris, the youngest, who found his mother dead one morning; the one who called 911; the one who had already suffered depression.

I looked up at our pastor Lowell, the first person we called after the police officers brought the unbelievable news. Lowell wore his robe, though it was a very warm, still day, the third of July. Our eyes met, his an intense, compassionate blue, mirroring his tender spirit. He knew about grief and not only professionally. He was caring for his wife and watching her slow decline due to Alzheimer's disease.

Behind him, faces illumined by tiny streaks of sunlight, were our friends, Marina and Teresa, guitarists who often accompanied Bill on Prison Fellowship trips to prisons. We had asked them to lead us in singing Claire's favorite songs and now they circulated song sheets to the gathered actors.

"I wonder if you could get me a hymnbook," Claire said one day. Unable to attend church due to constant pain, she read and marked her Bible; propped up, she sang in the night when she couldn't sleep.

"Here's my favorite," she said, " 'When I Survey the Wondrous Cross.' "

We sang that hymn and then another favorite, "I Am Covered Over with the Robe of Righteousness."

After prayers were offered, Lowell preached strong words of reassurance: "So it will be with the resurrection of the dead. The body that is sown is perishable; it is raised imperishable. It is sown in dishonor, it is raised in glory; it is sown in weakness, it is raised in power;

it is sown a natural body, it is raised a spiritual body." (I Cor. 15: 42-44) The two guitarists led us in the song "It Is Well with My Soul."

Claire's nieces and nephews placed flowers on her casket. And then my husband Bill stepped forward, his deep voice shaking, his arms outstretched: "Here Lord, I give you back the daughter you gave me."

Within me a fire began, a swelling of love and gratitude, and I joined him. I told the mourners in words I no longer remember how Claire would long for them to trust Christ if they had not done so.

As we stepped back, a wind began. It touched the edges of the lawn, it blew the women's skirts, and it rattled papers held in hands. And then the tree shook, branches bending, the leaves turning upward as if in praise. As quickly as it started, the wind withdrew and the leaves drooped.

Just before driving to the gravesite, our family had gathered together to view her body privately at the funeral home. Lesley had selected a bright red dress to bury her in, a color matching the energy, life, and spirit she had exhibited before her slow descent into pain and disability. Into the casket went a drawing of Jason's that his mother loved and her favorite photo of Christopher—the boys' choices. Chris had wanted to include her Bible, marked and highlighted, tear stained. But I told him, "You may want this someday."

The last addition was Claire's favorite stuffed puppy from childhood, a dog whose fur had been loved off and whose plaid patches were from my mother's sewing box.

When I entered the room I saw dozens of flower baskets surrounding the casket. There was a silence until I, the first in line, caught a glimpse of my daughter's beautiful face; I ran sobbing from the room.

She was really dead.

We hear a lot about denial, and perhaps that's where I was those first few days. Sometimes grief blanks out memory completely or is selective. Certain moments become fixed, like coming out of anesthesia where colors are brilliant and sounds amplified. Out of nowhere I relive the day after Claire's death with this snapshot: My husband is looking at a photo of our daughter as a little girl, standing next to her sister and wearing her winter coat with an Easter corsage. It was central New York, our home then. He is crying softly.

In his book, *Lament for a Son*, Nicholas Wolterstorff writes, "Why are the photographs of him as a little boy so incredibly hard for me to look at? Why is it easier to look at him as a grownup?"[1]

Our daughter was thirteen days shy of her forty-sixth birthday when she died. And I was seventy-one.

"For elderly parents who have no doubt known other losses, being predeceased by their child is intolerable and unnatural and produces a special sense of injustice and grief,"[2] write authors Joan Hagan Arnold and Penelope Buschman Gemma. And we sometimes fail to regard the grief of siblings, who have a special kind of lifelong relationship that is cut short.

When we first phoned Lesley in Indiana, she and Dick called their three daughters together. "We all sat in a circle, holding hands, crying, and praying," she told me later. "And Chico (their dog) pressed against me and howled right along with us."

I realized my son's pain when, after the funeral, I saw him crumpled over the sink, a casserole in hand, sobbing.

After our children and grandchildren left for their homes in Texas and Indiana, Bill and I dealt with the business of dying. There was no will and no money, only family antiques she had cherished. On disability for two years, she endured surgery, nerve blocks, and varieties of pills for her rib and back pain. Finally she was sent to a pain specialist who prescribed new, strong drugs. They seemed to help, she joyously proclaimed. But then one Saturday night the combination of prescription drugs stopped her heart.

Claire's disability had been caused by her spouse, who had never recovered from his experiences in Vietnam. During flashbacks he had attacked her repeatedly. Over the years since her separation from him, I had by God's grace been able to forgive him. But could I ever heal from her death?

One of my journal entries reads:

Two months have passed without Claire. Some days it seems unreal and impossible. Other days I feel I have accepted it. Sometimes I am frightened. It seems no matter how old your child, you should be there to protect her. That failed. Emptiness. She is gone. Hold my child close, Lord. You have taken her. Only recently could I say the words "Claire has died." I keep hearing those words in Bill's voice right after we received the news. They constrict my breathing; they tear apart my very being. It seems you are saying, "Renew your mind." My spirit is so sad. How shall I renew my mind? Give me your guidance.

In his book, *A Grace Disguised: How the Soul Grows Through Loss*, Gerald Sittser, who lost three family members in one car accident, says: "Sorrow never entirely leaves the soul of those who have suffered a severe loss. If anything, it may keep going deeper. But this depth of sorrow is the sign of a healthy soul, not a sick soul. It does not have to be morbid and fatalistic. It is not something to escape but something to embrace. Jesus said, "Blessed are those who mourn for they will be comforted!"[3]

I found that comfort in an unusual way. An early riser, I sat every morning facing the window, Bible or journal in hand, absorbing God's presence, imploring his mercy and grace, struggling daily to embrace my grief.

"My sheep hear my voice," Jesus said, and one morning, very early, I heard his voice, "Turn on the television." That didn't seem like a spiritual directive, but I had known him long enough to understand his ways weren't always mine. Over the years, I had identified that inner voice coming to me as a prompting, or sometimes in a dream.

I punched the remote and instantly a picture of grassy banks of sand and foamy seas moved to a background of music. Flamingoes stepped gracefully in rhythm. Superimposed was the scripture verse: "My soul finds rest in God alone; my salvation comes from him; he is my fortress, I will never be shaken." (Psalm 62:1,2)

That picture faded and another appeared: Unperturbed elk grazing at the foot of snow-covered mountains. Another verse, different music. For an hour in my recliner I feasted on the beauty of nature scenes from around the world, words of comfort for my soul. This continued daily for weeks. Then one morning a shouting evangelist appeared when I clicked my remote. But for then, it had been enough. Those peaceful mornings had steadied me as I began each day.

CHAPTER TWO

Faith & Flowers

Author with her parents

CHAPTER TWO

Faith & Flowers

I grew up in a brown-shingled house in central New York State that was adjacent to my father's nine greenhouses, the source of his livelihood. Through grimy panes of glass, passersby viewed beds of carnations and mums. Pots of poinsettias huddled together on splintery tables waiting for Christmas. Outside we were surrounded by profuse lilac bushes and rows of sturdy gladioli.

My childhood was peaceful. My parents were disciplinarians, although loving and generous. But I remember how early in life I longed for a brother or sister. My friends had siblings and I envied the fun and boisterous play when I visited their homes. I played hide-and-seek among the flowerbeds with my friends, crouching close to the dirt-packed floors of the humid greenhouses, scurrying behind two red banana trees transplanted from the tropics to the cold winters of New York State. Playtime included "selling" wilted flowers in our pretend store and chasing slithery but harmless black snakes around muddy corners.

My dad, a wholesale and retail grower in central New York State, spent long hours in his nine greenhouses pruning, cutting, and watering. Growing and selling occupied most of his time. I remember him crawling out of bed fully clothed during snowy nights to coal the hungry furnaces that kept the steam pipes hissing.

Since our vegetable garden and fruit trees yielded produce for my mother to can, cook, or pickle, I was expected to help. Potatoes, carrots, and beets were stored in our "root cellar." One job I hated was inspecting raspberries for worms; I found plenty. Plucking pinfeathers from fresh turkeys was another distasteful job.

My mother also spent much of her time working in the greenhouses and filling our house with fresh blooms—or those not quite good enough for customer flower arrangements. She grew hundreds of African violets, which she gave to friends and shut-ins.

One day as I watched her stir scrambled eggs and ham on our monstrous iron stove, I fed my doll at the table. "Here's your breakfast," I said to Gertrude, a 30s doll with composition face and cloth body. At six years old, I didn't understand much about "The Great Depression," but I knew that day after day ragged men appeared at our door asking for something to eat. This morning was no exception, and a man had knocked at our door. Mama cut thick slices of bread, spreading them with a layer of homemade jam. She spooned eggs on the plate, added a fork and then reached for the bouquet of roses on our kitchen table. Carefully selecting one, she placed it on the tray along with the plate of food and a mug of coffee.

Leaving Gertrude on a chair, I followed my mother to the back porch where a weary man leaned against the house, head hanging down.

"Here's your meal," my mother announced. "And here are soap and a towel if you'd like to wash up." She pointed to the hose by the door.

"Thank you, lady." He reached for the soap and towel but stopped at the sight of the tray. "A rose? Why, thank you! We had a rosebush once." He looked up, a stubble of gray beard from ear to ear. "A long time ago it was."

"Well, go ahead, wash and eat before your food gets cold," said Mama. "Just leave the tray there." She shut the door.

"Why did you give him a rose, Mama?" I asked.

My mother carried the frying pan to the sink. "Food feeds the body," she said, "but a rose, a rose feeds the soul."

Many of my father's customers saw only the beautiful part of our business. One tall lady, clasping her white-gloved hands together, exclaimed, "Oh, how wonderful it must be to work among the flowers!" My feisty father, pausing with mums in hand, replied, "Like to work spreading manure? How d'ya like working when it's 110 degrees in the house?"

Easter, Christmas, and Mother's Day caused bustling in the workroom. Dad dyed carnations green for St. Patrick's Day and sold dozens of red ones for Valentine's Day. Funerals meant not only arranged baskets and vases, but also tall standing crosses and enormous wreaths. Flowers and greens were wired one by one into damp mossy bases, handmade by employees. Easter corsages were not shipped already packed, as many are today, but crafted individually according to the order. Family and workers stayed up all night, completing the hundreds to be delivered early Easter morning. Even during Depression years, people had money for flowers. Sometimes, however, Dad received eggs or chickens as payment.

My father bought his bulbs directly from Holland. He pored over catalogs sent by the Dutch companies. Every year Mr. van Ruiten, a tall, distinguished Dutchman, came to our house, joining us for Mama's beef stew or roast duck and writing out Dad's order. Dad then checked it over with his father who, along with his wife, lived on the other side of the greenhouses.

Grandfather Ernest was born in Alsace-Lorraine and spoke only French when he arrived in America with his family. In 1873 he married Mary, who had emigrated from Germany with her mother Amelia and two sisters. During their courtship and throughout their marriage, English was the only means of communication since neither spoke the other's language. Their four children, my father included, never learned to speak either French or German. Two of the children died in their twenties of tuberculosis and appendicitis, but my father and Aunt Flora lived well past ninety.

Since our house and my grandparents' house were situated on either side of the family's greenhouses, I spent many hours in the gardens with Grandpa or in the house with Grandma, whose German and English Bibles always lay open on the massive dining room table.

Well into his eighties, Grandpa still participated in the business by separating and replanting cuttings. Over and over, row upon row, the plants were split and pressed into tiny containers. New life began all over again for each little shoot. I perched on a high wooden stool, short legs swinging above the rung, and watched him at the greenhouse "potting bench." Grandpa reached for my thumb and pressed it into the deep, sweet-smelling soil. "There, you've helped that little plant grow!" he announced.

My grandmother cut out strings of paper dolls or sewed doll clothes from paisley prints, putting touches of fur on the coat collars. One day when I brought my doll to be outfitted, Grandma pulled me to her knee and said, "Today you're going to learn the Lord's Prayer. "Our Father," she began slowly, "who art in heaven.…" Although only four or five at the time, I remember learning the prayer, repeating it several times with her.

Grandma read to me from the Bible as well, passages that told of God's love for us. "Remember," she told me, "Jesus is coming again!"

Later in life I learned that my grandmother's voyage to America had been filled with danger and death. For some unknown reason my great-grandmother had left her husband behind. Handwritten records read, "They had a bad trip; storms and mishaps were continuous. Twenty-two people died and were buried at sea. After eighty-two days on the water, they arrived in New York with all the masts broken and everything covered with ice." Wouldn't this have been a great adventure to share with your only grandchild? Yet Grandmother's favorite words were: "Jesus is coming again!"

In 1932, when I was seven, my grandparents died twelve hours apart. In that bustling, weeping household I was the only child. Adults went about their business whispering, weeping, making coffee, and serving crusty German kuchen, Aunt Flora's specialty.

Grandmother's collapse was due to Grandfather's illness and her death directly due to the hallucinatory raving of her dying husband. From his bedroom came the croaking sound, "Who is that woman? Get that woman out of here!"

I remember seeing sisters Amelia and Lydia helping Grandmother Mary from the room. Her hand to her chest, she collapsed into an ornate mahogany chair outside the door of death. I see her now, long skirts gathered together over a burgundy and gold cushioned seat, her head thrown back in a gesture of shock. Immediately, someone brought smelling salts. Then the picture fades. Her actual death, which was within minutes, and the death of my grandfather the next morning are forgotten; the next scene is my lone visitation to the two caskets positioned at right angles in the parlor. Curious, I stood on tiptoe, placing small hands on the satin edge of first one coffin, then the other. I could smell the giant baskets of flowers, and in the dim light (the shades were drawn), I looked up at the picture of Jesus kneeling in Gethsemane hanging on the wall behind the caskets. The rock on which his folded hands rested was made of glittery material that shone in the dark. I recall only a sense of quiet and peace.

In a box of clippings I found this yellowed newspaper account: *Man and Wife Die 12 Hours Apart After Living Together 59 Years.* In the reporting characteristic of the day, the obituary continued: "Mrs. Hermant died unexpectedly of a stroke of apoplexy at 8:10 last night, while her husband who had been ill since Friday died at 7:30 this morning of natural causes. He was 89 years old and his wife was 79. It was thought possible that Mrs. Hermant's collapse was due in part to the serious illness of Mr. Hermant. The latter died unaware that his wife had gone before him." I was listed as the single grandchild, for only my father had married, and then not until age thirty-nine.

In the few short years we were together, my German grandmother did not spend time telling me tales of her homeland she had left as a child or tales of the terrible crossing by sea, nor even stories of her mother who had had to start life over alone in a strange land. She didn't mention her son, Theodore, or her daughter, Leah, who died in their prime. Instead, she chose the times when she sewed for me to share her most important inheritance, her faith. She gave me the right roots, the roots of faith, and as I grew older, I knew that when our roots are in Christ, we understand our beginning and our eternal destiny. Our second birth is the new beginning for us.

If Grandma were living today, I know the verse she would read to me: "So then, just as you have received Christ Jesus as Lord, continue to live in him, rooted and built up in him, strengthened in the faith as you were taught, and overflowing with thankfulness." (Col. 2:6) And I'm sure she would add, "Jesus is coming again!"

Growing up among flowers and seeds, cuttings and plants produced a basis for teaching on spiritual growth. For example, as a
teenager, I often helped my father cover the beds of carnations with
black cloths to block out the summer evening light and fool the
plants into thinking it was night. This inhibited their flowering. As
an adult walking through life's dark places, I remembered the black
covers and their purpose in making the plants bloom more pro-
fusely.

Besides playing in the greenhouse, I roller skated, read piles of
books while snuggled in a wing chair, and wrote notebooks full of
stories. I played with our succession of cats. With no television then,
I listened to "Little Orphan Annie" on the radio and used my "de-
coder," a kid's early version of Game Boy. Although friends were
welcome in our home, I spent a lot of time alone and I enjoyed it,
but yet wished I had a brother or sister to share my feelings and
activities. I lifted my spirits by riding my bike to Lorraine's house, a
close friend who had four sisters and one brother. Always activity
there!

My greatest joy, though, was playing with my dolls. Every Christmas and birthday my parents bought me a different doll. No Barbies
then. No dolls that talked, walked, or wet. Gertrude, my favorite,
had very short hair due to my cleverness with scissors. There was a
big clown doll named Jack, redheaded Norma Jean, snuggly Ruth
Doris and Baby Jane. With their faces cracked, fingers missing and
tummies split open to expose cotton batting, these dolls were too
well loved to become collectibles.

Grandma Mary sewed for hours to provide my dolls with styl-
ish wardrobes. She knew how much I loved my dolls. I shared con-
fidences with them, read to them, lined them up and lectured them.
These dolls were hugged, smelled, and kissed, and pushed in a wicker
carriage.

When I grow up, I thought, I'll have babies to love. I'll never
ever have an only child, and I'll love my children forever.

CHAPTER THREE

A Yankee Goes South

Author with fiance Bill in uniform

CHAPTER THREE

A Yankee Goes South

One Sunday afternoon in December 1941, while I was rehearsing a play at my high school, the door to the auditorium swung open, banging against the wall as a schoolmate stumbled toward the stage shouting, "We're at war! The Japanese have attacked Pearl Harbor!" What immediately followed is lost to my memory, but the event changed America forever. And it changed the direction and decisions of my own life.

War was already part of our lives with Hitler's braggadocio and monstrous invasions a reality reported in our newspapers and seen on "Movietone News." But America observed it from a distance, as though a canyon separated us from the evildoers. Now we would offer up our young men, manufacture war machinery, and ration our food and gasoline. We would fight an enemy most of us had only seen in the movies.

For a year I had been corresponding with two nieces of my father's Dutch bulb salesman, who told me they had been robbed of their valuables under the Nazi occupation. They were so hungry that they cooked bulbs for food. Their precious letters, censored with black ink and stamped with the Nazi swastika, have been lost over the years. Somehow this mail arrived, however, and our family mailed them packages of essentials—tea, coffee, stockings, and even bicycle tires—which, only by God's grace, were not stolen or confiscated.

Mr. van Ruiten's niece, Joop, who married Jaap de Groot, stopped writing to me in 1968 because she could no longer write in English, but when Lesley studied in Europe between college semesters, she celebrated her twenty-first birthday at the de Groot home. Then last year I located Joop through the Internet and wrote to her. Her daughter Maria translated her letter back to me, enclosing a recent photo of her mother. Though we had never met we had "known" each other for over sixty years.

At the time of the Pearl Harbor attack, my boyfriend Bill had entered a two-year agricultural and technical school in Canton, New York. Bill and I met in church and had gone steady for three years. After graduating, he was sworn into the Army in December 1942 and trained as a radio repairman in the Signal Corps School at Ft. Monmouth, New Jersey.

With the escalation of the war and Bill in the service, I changed my educational focus. Originally planning to take journalism at Cornell, I enrolled instead at a radio and theater school in Boston for one year. As a teenager, I had acted and broadcasted from a local radio station, and I decided to spend this year training for work in radio, not knowing then that I would eventually work in television as well.

While he was home on furlough, Bill and I decided to marry as soon as possible. "I might not come home," he told me solemnly. "Or without an arm or a leg. Or even I might not be able to have children." Like millions of other couples who were dating or engaged, young people who loved each other and perceived a life of faith, work, and family ahead of them, Bill and I matured quickly. As Tom Brokaw says in his book *The Greatest Generation*, "They answered the call to save the world from the two most powerful and ruthless machines ever assembled, instruments of conquest in the hands of fascist maniacs."[4]

Plans for school or jobs dissolved quickly. Our country needed us, and the draft accelerated. We thought we were ready—strong, patriotic, mission-driven—but we could never have anticipated the massive death and destruction that lay ahead. We couldn't know of the Bataan Death March or the D-Day invasion or the first use of the atomic bomb.

During a furlough in December 1944, Bill and I were married in the church where we had met as part of the youth group. After a short and frugal honeymoon to New York City, Bill left for Warner Robins Air Force Base in Georgia. By that time I had finished my year at school and had a job in the local radio station writing copy and hosting programs. I lived with my parents, sleeping in my childhood bed and saving money from my paycheck and my government allowance as a serviceman's wife.

Then in May of 1945 the radio station gave me a month off to join Bill at the base camp before he shipped out. This was the war-time forties, and Georgia, like many other Southern states, seemed stuck in the post-Civil War era. A Yankee girl who grew up in the fierce winters and pleasant summers of New York, I had traveled with my parents to the beaches of Maine, the mountains of New Hampshire, to Quebec and Montreal. But I had never visited the South, let alone a hot, dusty state like Georgia, whose red clay soil clung to my socks and shoes. I couldn't understand people's speech or their lifestyles; I particularly couldn't understand that the "colored" were treated like Dickensian children, punished, segregated, even cheated.

My journey from New York to Georgia was not by plane or by car, not even by Greyhound or Amtrak. My only way to travel then was to ride coach on an old train, battered by time and devoid of conveniences or meals. The better trains were transporting troops. I carried snacks for thirty-six hours and sat up in a coach seat along with an assortment of other tired travelers, including servicemen who had been on furlough.

The long trip was worth it. As the train brakes screeched, I looked out the window and there he was, my soldier in uniform, waving his hat wildly in the air.

Our first home as newlyweds was a room in the barracks furnished with two olive-drab army cots, a bar on which to hang clothes, and two "dressers" made out of orange crates. Barren furnishings didn't matter; we were together. We pushed the cots next to each other and opened the windows of course. There was no air conditioning or fan and the May heat in Georgia was stifling.

George, Abe, and Marvin were three of Bill's buddies, and I soon became acquainted with their wives who told me the one perk of living on base was a swimming pool for servicemen's families.

I wasn't sure if it was a perk for me or not. I couldn't swim and suffered a great fear of water since a near-drowning incident in childhood. Years ago, while at Rockaway Beach in Long Island with my parents, I had met a twelve-year-old boy who boasted that he could teach anyone to swim. A naive ten-year-old, I followed him into the crashing waves and before long he pulled me under and held me down. When I finally surfaced, choking and sputtering, I lay on the beach so frightened I felt I would never go in the water again.

As a nineteen-year-old Yankee in Georgia, I wanted to fit in. After our husbands left our barrack's rooms for the day, we wives washed their uniforms, and hung them to dry until we ironed them the next day. Besides no air conditioning, there were no washers or dryers. As a reward for our hard work, we headed for the pool, books and towels in hand. These new friends were determined to teach me to swim and I felt this was my chance to learn. Their concern for me made me all the more determined to overcome this fear and learn to stay afloat and even to swim as well as they could. I struggled as they held their arms under me, coaching and encouraging. But one day the girls pulled me out of the water quickly.

"What's the matter?" I asked.

"You're white as a sheet!" one gasped, helping me to the side of the pool. "I guess this isn't going to work."

Embarrassed, I wondered if they were fed up with me. I made up my mind that I would try again.

I persisted, and finally learned to float on my back. The ability left me after my days in Georgia. I don't understand why. I really wanted to learn, and later, when I had a family, I made sure that each child had swimming lessons early in life.

Daily I spread my army-issue bath towel on the cement by the pool, pillow wadded under my head, absorbing the sun. No one talked of danger from sunbathing in those days, and since I was used to sunning by Adirondack lakes or on Maine beaches, I was unprepared for the scorching May sun in the Deep South.

One day at the pool I lay dreaming, dozing, or reading for over three hours. Not only did sunburn result, but sun poisoning with fever and chills. My white thighs were red and covered with giant blisters. I didn't go to the infirmary, but carefully snuggled in my husband's arms while watching a movie on base. First feeling hot, then cold, I finally recovered and sunned again, covering my thighs and my feet.

As the weeks passed, our awareness of the separation soon to come became the focus of our time together. We knew he was headed for the Pacific Theater.

Only nineteen and twenty, Bill and I had grown up in hard-working middle-class families, attending the same church on Sundays, but understanding very little about true worship. Both Bill and I had committed our lives to Christ while at church camp at Oak Point on the St. Lawrence River. Singing around the campfire and listening to our leader, I wondered if I was being called to the mission field. That's how real my commitment felt. Soon after that, I was asked to "entertain" at a program for the women of our church. Popular in the '30s and '40s was the monologue, an early form of stand-up comedy. I memorized some of the work of a famous monologist, Cornelia Otis Skinner, but I also wrote some of my own copy.

After I finished my monologue, I bowed to the laughter and clapping of my audience. As soon as it died down, I heard a man's booming voice from the door of our fellowship hall. Dressed in black and waving an even blacker Bible, the missionary called out to me: "Young woman, with a voice like that, you should be reading to us from the Psalms!"

For weeks the voice and the exhortation rang in my head. Was God speaking to me?

CHAPTER FOUR

Baby Time

Author's three children, Claire on left

CHAPTER FOUR

Baby Time

After three years in the Air Force, Bill came home, and he came home whole, full of stories but free of injury since he did not see action. After he left Georgia, he was based at Hickam Field in Honolulu where he installed and maintained blind landing systems on bombers.

As we settled into post World War II life, we worked hard, saved every cent possible and immediately planned a family. It took me almost a year to get pregnant for our first baby, and I cried every month when I discovered no baby had been conceived. Children! I wanted them! And of course more than one. It took time, but later on in life I loved hearing the question, "Do you have children?" I could smile and say, "Yes, we have three."

However, bringing up our three children proved to be different than caring for dolls. My dolls sat where I put them, never talked back or cried, needed no food and slept quietly all night. For help, I, like many members of my generation of mothers, read Dr. Spock's *Baby and Child Care.* I went to Dr. Spock frequently and listened to my mother and mother-in-law.

Each generation has its own rules: to spank or not to spank; to let them cry or pick them up; to take away the bottle or let them keep it. Although Dr. Spock's advice changed somewhat over the years, one bit of advice probably saved my daughter, Claire's, life.

One sunny morning in September, I heard cries from Claire's crib and noises of vomiting. Rushing into the room, I saw an arc of vomit from the crib soar across the room. At once Dr. Spock's words echoed through my mind: "The food is vomited out with great force so that it lands a distance from the baby's mouth. It usually needs immediate medical attention."

Today, I would have scooped up the child and headed for the ER. But then, in simpler and quieter days, we counted on the doctor to come to our home. Shaking, I phoned Dr. Kaplan at his home. "It's Claire!" I shouted. "She has projectile vomiting and a fever!"

Although it was not yet seven o'clock and Bill had left for work, our pediatrician didn't hesitate. "I'll be right there. We need to get her to the hospital."

Lesley, our five-year-old, had gone to bed the night before excited about her first day of kindergarten. What should I do? Quickly I woke her to dress and hauled out cereal as I phoned a neighbor to ask if her older daughter could walk my child to her very first day of school.

When the doctor arrived, Claire, only two years old, asked him if she could bring her puppy—a brown plush dog she had received for her birthday. The same stuffed animal would one day lie gently against her in her final resting place.

"Sure," he answered. "Let's go." He hustled us into his car.

Dr. Spock's advice was the first thing to save Claire's life; otherwise, I would not have understood the danger of "projectile" vomiting. The second was the discovery of intravenous feeding. In these days of ultrasound, angiograms, and MRIs, it's hard to believe that a simple procedure of IVs was a fairly new medical discovery. Into a tiny arm a nurse inserted the needle. "Don't hurt! Don't hurt me!" my baby cried out.

As I sat by her crib in the hospital, I saw color return to her pale cheeks and the vomiting cease. Severe dehydration had almost taken her life. My heart thumped with relief.

But it was not over. The third day when I returned to the room, a nurse's aide smiled at me as she held Claire under the arms. Sitting on a potty in her crib, Claire's head hung down; her body was limp.

"She's such a good little thing," said the aide. "Not a whimper out of her."

One look at my baby and I knew she wasn't being "good." Something was seriously wrong. My heart, already strained with the fear of losing my child, now seemed to swell, grow, almost burst.

It took five seconds of sprinting to reach the nurse's station. "It's my baby!" I hollered. "I think she's in a coma!"

Starched uniforms stirred quickly. The IVs were started once again, in her thighs now since her little arms were well punctured.

This time it took longer for change, but change did come: pink cheeks, movement, speech. As I stayed near her, my friend Betty, a nurse, came in to visit. Hearing the story and looking at me she said, "I'm staying with her tonight. You'll go home and sleep. I won't leave her side."

That night, awake, talking with Bill and my mother, I felt strong and thankful. But alone later in the middle of the night I sat by the window, crying and praying. I don't remember the words I used, but I sensed God's comfort.

The day after Claire's birth, my florist father had brought a bouquet of flowers with a card that read: "To Claire Louise—welcome to my new sister from Lesley Jane." Claire's newborn eyes seemed to focus on the flowers. "My sweet flower girl," I murmured, kissing her.

Coming close to losing my child caused me to take a closer look at our family life. What would it be like to say goodbye to a two-year-old who was just beginning to talk, to ride her tricycle, to play with her dolls?

At home, dressing to go back to the hospital, I moved into the girls' bedroom, looked at Claire's empty bed and fell down beside it. "God, God," I sobbed, unable to form words. My thoughts were fearful, agonized. I didn't know anyone whose child had died, and I dared not think of that, lest I bring it about.

Lesley had survived her first days at school without a mommy or daddy to ask questions, to praise, to encourage. But even now in middle age, she remembers that important first day with a neighbor child holding her hand as she walked down the street and up the steps to her new world.

Always in the back of my mind was the desire for more children. As they were growing up, our children remember me stepping in when their fighting became intense, grabbing hold to reprimand them: "You don't know how lucky you are to have brothers and sisters!"

Since I never liked being an only child, I felt I had given my children a precious gift—each other.

Bill wanted another baby, too, especially a chance to have a son. But I didn't conceive easily and my first delivery had been difficult and traumatic. Finally I became pregnant and when Claire was four-and-a-half, I gave birth to a nine-pound four-ounce boy the day after Christmas.

It was the fifties, a time when mothers seldom worked outside the home. Housework was time-consuming. Few people had dryers or dishwashers. Microwaves had not been invented. An occasional family had black-and-white television and we were one of them.

Bill worked for General Electric, and his hobby was amateur ham radio. When he left work, he called me on the radio to tell me he was on the way home and I would have supper ready. I scrubbed, starched, ironed, baked, and washed cloth diapers. Being housebound with the care of three small children, I no longer found time to read or write, my favorite pursuits. Both sets of grandparents lived in our city and occasionally helped out.

With the addition of a new baby and a boy at that, Claire showed signs of jealousy. Never a demanding child, she cried for attention and refused food. Worried, I took her to our family doctor who asked to talk to her alone.

"She's caught in the middle," he told me. "She has a new baby brother everyone fusses over, and she can't do all the things her older sister is allowed to do."

I seldom left the house alone. One night the stress caught up with me. I was attending a meeting at my daughter's neighborhood school. While taking notes and listening to discussions, I felt heat rising from my toes to my head. My breathing constricted; I suddenly felt as though I were a rocket taking off into space. My pencil dropped and I held my face in my hands. Through roaring in my ears, I heard the man next to me say "I'm taking you home. I know

what you're going through. I've been there. Come on, just leave
your car here."

I frightened Bill. As an asthmatic, he watched me gasping and
thought I was having a similar attack. An attack it was, but not
what Bill thought.

I lived through what I can only describe as a three-month-long
panic attack. How easily we talk and read today about anxiety, psy-
chosis, post-partum depression, bi-polar disease, paranoia, schizo-
phrenia. In those days, everything was characterized (at least by the
layman) as a "nervous breakdown" or "being crazy." As a teenager, I
remember passing a house near my grandmother's and seeing a retarded or demented man peering out of a window. "He's a crazy
man," I was told. His family had hidden him away, locked him in
an attic bedroom, ashamed of his appearance and behavior. Today
he would be in a special education class, seeing a counselor, medi-
cated, and taken to church, properly cared for.

But these were different times, and even in the fifties, anti-de-
pressants were still unknown and tranquilizers were just coming on
the market. My gynecologist prescribed one of these new drugs, not
knowing this should only be given for serious psychoses.

Insomnia gripped me. My stomach lurched constantly, tighten-
ing my rib cage. The few nights I could fall asleep I would awaken
in the morning, lying still, noticing that my insides were quiet. But
then, gradually, the demon would seize me again and the rolling
and tugging began. "No, no!" I would cry. "Please, God, stop it!"
While my family slept, I would stumble downstairs and walk the
floor, fast, faster, faster, moaning and crying.

Looking back I can only imagine the fear my husband and parents felt. I continued to care for the house and the children. My
mother would come over some mornings after my sleepless nights
so I could go back to bed. Even then, sleep would not come. I tried
hot baths, cold baths, and wrapping myself in a blanket. One day,
sleep deprived and wild with anxiety, I grabbed a rake and attacked
the leaves in the yard, thinking strenuous activity would calm the
demon.

Even though my thoughts were self-centered and consuming, I feared for the children's well being. I had a baby to dress and feed properly, though I seemed to have no trouble caring for him. Lesley was in school. But what of Claire, a sensitive and perceptive child, who was at home with me all day? I could not sit to read stories or play for I was fighting a turbulent force inside of me that would not let me go. Would the change in her mother affect her adversely? This only added to my guilt and distress.

Bill had added home responsibilities now, with housework and the care of our children. One night he cried, "I don't know how much more of this I can take. I feel like I'm losing my mind, too."

Today I'm sure that Xanax® or a similar drug would have helped me recover, along with counseling to see what might have been at the bottom of my anxiety. My pastor tried to help me, but although he prayed, he also told me his wife was depressed and often sat up on a bank of pillows all night.

I knew my close friends did not understand this; my family didn't understand it; probably outsiders called me "crazy." But then one morning I looked in my bedroom mirror and saw another woman, someone I didn't recognize. Surely this couldn't be me! I wanted to lash out, to strike her, and make her disappear.

The drug I was taking had altered my mental state disastrously. Today's information on this particular drug accurately describes my condition: "…may cause an unusual increase in psychotic symptoms or may cause paranoid reactions. It may also cause suicidal thoughts."

Another doctor who saw me then was astounded that I had been given such a strong drug. I was put on a mild tranquilizer, and soon after the nightmare ended as quickly as it started. One morning I awakened without anxiety.

I was me again.

CHAPTER FIVE

A Yankee Goes South—Again

*Author with First Lady Pat Nixon
at the White House*

CHAPTER FIVE

A Yankee Goes South—Again

Now that one of my three precious children has died, now that I am a great-grandmother, I sometimes sit on my apartment balcony, reflecting on the turning points in my life. My path of life has been a long journey strewn with flowers and weeds, and sometimes, barren land. Early in life it was a slow journey as the days dragged by and physical labor and childcare marked each day. But as people of age attest, time speeds by as we near our destination—eternal life.

The walk is now faster, but when did it become different for me, more meaningful? I trace the time back to 1973 when people from all Christian traditions in our area gathered in homes, in churches, in schools, in coffee shops. These gatherings grew like wild fire, and indeed it was the fire of the Holy Spirit pointing people to lives of prayer and praise and implanting a hunger for the Word of God.

Thousands began to ask themselves the questions Bill and I asked: Is this all there is? Is there more to worship than sitting or kneeling in a pew, reciting a creed only in your head? Is there more than a half-hearted attempt to sing a hymn? Does your mind wander during a sermon? Did God really mean "You shall love me with all your heart, with all your soul and with all your strength"? (Deut. 6:5)

For years we had heard rumbles of revival in various churches and Christian faith traditions. We had been raised in church and read the Bible, but our faith lacked vitality. We knew about the Trinity, but the teaching of the Holy Spirit's work was absent.

During this time in our lives, Claire attended three years of art school. During the summer she worked in a florist shop, forming bouquets and corsages into the flower designs she envisioned. It made me think of the time my five-year-old "flower girl" picked violets and brought them to me as a special gift.

After Claire had graduated from art school, she married a veteran of the Vietnam War. A year later she delivered a stillborn baby girl. Soon after this tragedy, Claire drove in from her home in Charlottesville to spend a few days with us, and we encouraged her to go with us to a prayer and praise meeting at Vic and Dorothy Aderton's home.

There was no need to ring the doorbell. People crowded the entrance two or three at a time, hugging and trying to move inside so others behind them could get in the door. The porch light flickered and bugs swarmed crazily around the entrance. Almost forty people had gathered in the house, notebooks and Bibles in hand. Some were from mainline denominations; there were Pentecostals, Evangelicals, and Catholics.

"Here are some chairs, back here," Dorothy motioned. Vic hurried out of the room to get more. Men and women were sitting on the staircase, others knee-to-knee on a sofa with straight chairs wedged in next to upholstered. A few teenagers sat on the fireplace hearth, but most of the gathering consisted of people career-age or older.

That night we prayed, we studied our Bibles with our leader encouraging us; we sang songs of praise and worship. Then it was time for ministry to each other, a new concept in our lives. People wept freely, submitting themselves to the touch of others and to the prayers of faith. Claire sat in a chair, surrounded by loving people who knew about her baby's death. She, too, wept as she opened her heart to Christ. But then joy erupted as she felt released from her pain and the Spirit began to work.

We had moved to Lynchburg, Virginia, in 1959 with our three children, a company move for Bill: new house, new schools, new friends for all of us. Here I was again, a Yankee wife and now a mom transported to a sleepy, proper, and preppie southern town. Arriving at the beginning of the civil rights movement, we soon found that no Yankees were welcome in this quiet, provincial community whose ancestors had settled along the James River.

Most of the residents had grown up here, building solid homes, their massive columns and turrets daring entrance. Some were Federal style, others Gothic, Greek revival, Georgian, Victorian. The wealthier mansions had sometimes housed generations of families. Closer to Main Street, and fanning out from historical districts, were frame houses, some in good repair, others not, housing black families whose fathers, if any, worked in steamy industries, textile or shoe factories, and whose mothers set off daily on buses to clean or cook for white families. Their children attended segregated schools, "separate but equal."

Genteel ladies shopped in the only place in those days, downtown, dressed in designer skirts and white gloves, assisted by mannerly sales people whose incomes may have forced them to work, or whose desire to serve others expressed itself in retail business.

Into this climate moved hundreds of families, Yankees from New York and New England, whose heritage was every bit as proud as the people of the South, their Revolutionary past and their historical sites cherished. Both General Electric and Babcock and Wilcox were expanding their facilities in the South. These transferred families built the new style homes of the fifties and sixties, solid brick ranches or split levels, spaced neatly on new lots separate from the long-established properties of the native inhabitants. They brought money and business talents to the community, white children for the white schools, and religious members for the profuse number of churches.

Years later this combining of North and South would be welcomed as the merging of people of color, people of faith, people of good will. We would begin to understand each other even when tempers flared and eruptions occurred. But at the time of our move, the War Between the States still caused animosity. And what, I thought, would my new southern friends think if they knew the North still admired General William Tecumseh Sherman who sacked and burned the city of Richmond?

Since Bill had left military service and begun work for General Electric, "getting ahead" was his goal. He believed in looking out for Number One and attaining status in the business world by his own strength. His big physical size, his deep voice, and profane vocabulary all helped him get what he wanted.

Before and after we moved, Bill held offices in our church as well as leadership roles in civic organizations. He had "power" in his life, but it was not from the Holy Spirit. It was worldly power, negative and cold. He knew who Christ was and what Christ had done, but he thought attending church and "serving" as an officer or leader underscored his business abilities and set an example for our children.

After our move to Virginia, we went to church of course. Wasn't that the right thing to do? The services we attended extolled the trappings of Christianity, but not a personal Savior.

With our children older and in school, I had time once again to read and write, but with college on the horizon for our oldest, I decided to look for a job in radio, where I had trained as a young woman. The television station had recently been sold to a Washington, DC, firm, and the building housed a radio station as well. After applying for a copy-writing job, I met a whirlwind producer who snatched me out of a chair and asked if I could host a television program. I wasn't sure, but with drama and writing background, I said I could try. Immediately I was on trial, positioned opposite two staff members and instructed, "Go ahead and interview them."

Hired the next day, I began to write and produce a daily black-and-white television program of local news, interviews, demonstrations, and the occasional celebrity appearance, one of whom I remember fondly. She was Julie Nixon, a presidential daughter whose engagement to David Eisenhower had recently been a matter of press. Securing the building before her entrance were three Secret Service men, one of whom asked me to "go easy" on her, as it was "her time of the month." The television host of "Good Morning America," Charles Gibson, began his career as the news reporter on my show.

I faced the camera Monday through Friday, after making sure my makeup was camera-ready, false eyelashes on straight and my sixties' hairpiece in place. My life became hectic as I taped for radio and television, promoted products, and challenged politicians. We went to church most Sundays, but who had time to read the Bible or pray during the week?

I talked to God though. "I know you don't approve of this," I told him one morning as I combed my hair before a studio mirror. "This" was an interview I was about to do that compromised my values and ethics. "But," I added, "I'm going to do it anyway!" How could I have been so blind?

The Holy Spirit began to work in us when a friend who lost his job did not seem upset about it. "How can you be so peaceful about this?" we asked Paul. Instead of answering, he invited us to go with him and his wife to a Bible study. As we joined them weekly at Vic and Dorothy's, we found we were not the only ones seeking "something more."

We read in the Book of the Prophet Amos a truth that was happening in our time: "'The days are coming,'" says the sovereign Lord, 'when I will send a famine through the land—not a famine of food or a thirst for water, but a famine of hearing the words of the Lord.'" (Amos 8:11)

As we dusted off our Bibles to study and as we sought the Lord in prayer, we felt a new excitement, different from what the world offers. Here were answers, guidance, and piercing reminders of the commitments we had once made to Christ.

When we came face to face with ourselves in God's Word, we were stunned. "Here I am!" I told Bill, as I read the Parable of the Sower in Matthew 13. "I'm the one who Jesus says hears the word which is the seed, but when it fell among thorns, those thorns grew up and choked the word. And Jesus said, 'What was sown among the thorns is the man who hears the word, but the worries of this life and the deceitfulness of wealth choke it, making it unfruitful.'"

Bill's life was expressed in Jeremiah 17 and throughout the remainder of his life he would share this with others:

This is what the LORD says:
"Cursed is the one who trusts in man,

who depends on flesh for his strength
and whose heart turns away from the LORD.
He will be like a bush in the wastelands;
he will not see prosperity when it comes.
He will dwell in the parched places of the desert,
in a salt land where no one lives.
"But blessed is the man who trusts in the LORD,
whose confidence is in him.
He will be like a tree planted by the water
that sends out its roots by the stream.
It does not fear when heat comes;
its leaves are always green.
It has no worries in a year of drought
and never fails to bear fruit."

We marveled at how God uses his creation to express truths for us. The Parable of the Sower ends this way: "But what was sown on good soil is the man who hears the word and understands it. He produces a crop, yielding a hundred, sixty, or thirty times what was sown."

As we joyfully rededicated our lives to Jesus, changes occurred. My new commitment made me evaluate what I produced on television and what I said on a daily radio commentary. Did it glorify God by being truthful? Did it promote his principles? And Bill found new guidelines for his job and his relationships. He became sensitive to others, including his children and me.

Another change in my life was an inner transformation that would be wrought in valleys, not mountaintops. Our gracious God, who knew me from the beginning and veiled his eyes in pain as I rebelled, knew what lay ahead of us. Without the mercy of Jesus' personal touch in my life, I might have gone under, unable to cope with the trials that lay ahead: unwed pregnancies in our family, children's divorces, the long-term care of aging parents, the death of two infant grandchildren and the death of my daughter, Claire.

CHAPTER SIX

His Perfect Love

Claire as a child

CHAPTER SIX

His Perfect Love

While going through Claire's files and papers after her death, I found a hand-written essay about her faith called "His Perfect Love." Crafted years after the night she went with us to that prayer and praise meeting, it shows the lifelong presence of Christ in her life that was validated by the loving people who surrounded her. I am sorry that my own mother, the grandmother in this writing, never saw this piece.

Claire wrote:

It was long ago when the Lord first showed me his perfect love. In fact I was no more than five years old. Although I am now a forty-year-old mother of two teen-age boys, I remember the incident so distinctly that it seems only moments since I experienced it. I have recalled it untold times for reassurance and inspiration to continue the struggle of living.

It was Easter Sunday and my family attended Olivet Presbyterian Church in Utica, New York, as we did every Sunday. I was proud of my new bonnet with the blue velvet trim. I was certain it was admired by all. My sister was sporting her new black patent leather shoes. My brother, a baby, was dressed in his best outfit with a cap to match. My mother and grandmother wore orchid corsages provided by my grandfather, who was a florist. My father, an imposing 6' 3" looked so regal in his best blue suit. I remember the over-polished oak pews that threatened to toss me and my crinolines to the floor. There were beautiful white lilies everywhere.

I always sat next to my grandmother, whom I dearly loved. The love she showed me was my first encounter with unconditional love. My parents certainly loved me unconditionally but parent/child relationships are complex and differ from the kind of relationship a child has with a grandparent. She smelled like the violets she raised and she always wore a rather intimidating fox stole complete with snout, feet, and glassy eyes. I assumed my parents never told Grandmother of my many misdeeds since she accepted me completely and seemed to perceive me as flawless. I enjoyed sitting next to her every Sunday. She would slip me peppermint Life Savers and never give me a stern look of disapproval if I wiggled and fidgeted.

This day was special. I wanted to be part of the celebration. "Hallelujah, Hallelujah," I sang at the top of my voice. I listened intently while our pastor told us of the extraordinary sacrifice God made for us. He gave his only Son to die an agonizing death that we might live with him forever. He took our sins upon him and shed his blood for me. I marveled at the idea that Jesus would die for me. I stared at the rough-hewn wood cross draped in purple. It was put up in front of the sanctuary every Easter, yet somehow today it seemed different. I tried to picture in my young mind what it would feel like to be nailed to that cross. The nails they drove through Jesus' hands and feet surely hurt more than getting a finger caught in the spokes of my tricycle. As I thought of these things, everything around me became distant. I focused my attention on that wooden cross. Ever so slowly I slid up in my pew and ever so carefully so as not to be noticed, I stretched my small arms out wide. I closed my eyes as I imagined myself on the cross. Suddenly I felt pleasantly warm and filled with a contentment that is beyond words even now. As small as I was, I knew I was experiencing the love of Christ. He wanted me to know of his love for me! For those brief moments I was bathed in perfect love and acceptance.

Even the love of my grandmother paled by comparison. It was a profound and unforgettable experience. I became aware of my grandmother's arms around me, bringing me gently back down beside her. She kissed the top of my head and held me close. I opened my eyes, peeked again at that rough wooden cross. I felt myself smiling, as I knew I had experienced something very special. There were no words, no explanation for a child of five to relate. I told no one and kept my secret close to my heart for many years. I have known since that moment that I must belong to him, that his love for me is essential as I encounter the struggles of this life. I have sought his face countless times through the years. I have turned to Him and been assured that He is there for me. Managing the anguish and shame of a traumatic divorce, He was there to give me strength. In the midst of the painful loss of a baby son and a daughter He was there to give me blessed comfort. During the twelve years of single parenting, working full time, exhausted and emotionally spent, He is there with encouragement and assurance of his love for me. Burdened by seemingly impossible finances, He creatively covers my need. Overwhelmed at times by the special needs of two children, He reminds me that He can endure it for me. Through years of chronic pain He replaces my despair with hope. Unconditional love. I continue to learn of his love. He loves me the same now as when He revealed his love for me at age five. How exquisitely He cares for me!

My grandmother is gone now and many years have passed since that wonderful day. Grandmother introduced me to unconditional love and we continued to enjoy a special relationship until her death at age ninety. Her love and total acceptance of me whether we were picking strawberries or going through her immense button collection paved the way for me to accept God's love and forgiveness.

The process of growing up is a long and arduous journey for both child and parents. Along with the confusion and doubt as we develop is the need to be loved and accepted. Our first understanding of love comes, hopefully, from our parents and grandparents. We test that love repeatedly for assurance. Children are never too young to hear of God's love for them. My experience as a young child convinces me how important it is to fill the needs of our children. They need to know Jesus. They are open and eager to know how much He cares for them. How they need this assurance in preparation for life's difficult journey.

Jesus said, "Let the little children come to me and do not hinder them for the Kingdom of Heaven belongs to such as these." (Matt. 19:14)

We cannot ignore this command. Our children must be prepared and equipped to meet the challenges and difficult decisions life will demand of them. How can we send them into a world today full of destructive and deviant alternatives without knowing the Savior?

Not everyone was brought up in a loving home. Too many felt rejected and unloved. In fact you may feel that you are unlovable, not deserving love because you are unacceptable in some way. Even the best parents (most committed?) send messages of disapproval and rejection at times. We are all human and do not love one another with the perfect love of Christ Jesus. The Good News is we can lay these burdens that have oppressed us for so long at the foot of the Cross. He will then carry them for us. Jesus longs to reveal his love and acceptance of us just as we are. Not until we receive his love and forgiveness can we love and forgive others and be released from the bondage of hurt and unforgiveness.

Seek his face and open your heart to the perfect love of Jesus. Only then are we free to love others and live fully.

When I first found this so soon after she died, my grief ballooning in my chest, I didn't know whether to rail at God for taking my daughter away, or bless him for giving me such a loving, creative child. The tension seemed overwhelming. I felt torn in half, like a piece of cloth that has been ripped apart. Threads dangle from each half, but can never be woven back into the same piece. The part of me that related to my daughter—that intimacy—had taken a death-blow.

In their book, *Five Cries of Grief,* about the loss of their son, A. Irene Strommen expresses my feelings: "(I have) lost part of myself, as well as part of my motherhood, part of my self-image, part of my self-identity. It stands to reason that when a child dies, a mother is forced to come to grips with aspects of her own identity."[5]

Someone said to me soon after Claire's death, "But you still have two wonderful children." That is true, but not helpful during grief. If I lost an arm, would you say to me, But you still have the other arm and two legs?

Now, distanced from that time of loss, I can look back and process that period differently. Loss changed my life forever, but with God's grace, a smooth sea now surrounds me; the waves no longer wash over me, only ripples remain; the fire of suffering does not consume me. (Isa. 43:2)

Memories come and go, both frightening and comforting, both heartbreaking and warming. Not only was my daughter a woman of faith, but a woman of joy and humor, the humor her family remembers when we gather together.

CHAPTER SEVEN

A Joke a Day

Illustration by Claire

A Joke a Day

After having surgery on my nose for a deviated septum, Claire
sent me this poem in a paper shaped like a red bulbous nose.
There once was a woman I knew
Whose nose she continually blew;
When after repair
She sniffed at the air,
And said, "The old is preferred
To the new!"

No matter what the circumstances, my daughter's sense of humor bubbled over into poems, cartoons, and jokes. My father wrote
stories and limericks too, but for him time to write was limited.
Since we lived next door to the greenhouses, he was always "on
call." And the business, although dealing with flowers, required much
repair and use of tools for roofing, window glazing, truck motors,
cement work, wooden flower beds; the list was long and Dad's tool
collection was extensive, some of which ended up in Bill's workshop. Both men and then our son possessed a talent for working
with their hands.

Claire often commented on her father's "mentoring" in his
workshop. From the time she was small, the two of them spent
many hours cutting, using saws and drills, standing over the
Shopsmith®. "It didn't matter to Dad that I was a girl," she told
me. "He taught me how to use tools safely, how to turn and cut,
shape, and paint."

"Claire's the creative one," her brother and sister used to say.
But what is creativity? Is it inherited or is environment the bigger
contributor? Philosophers and psychologists ponder this and report
their differing beliefs. But isn't creativity a way of thinking that expresses itself in countless forms? Looking back at Lesley and Wayne's

lives, I see these forms: gifts of organization and leadership, gifts of speaking and compassion. James in the Bible says, "Every good and perfect gift is from above, coming down from the Father of the heavenly lights, who does not change like shifting shadows." (1:17) Our God is the Creator, and we are fashioned according to his plan. Our part comes in nurturing what our Creator has bestowed upon us.

From an early age, Claire's observations of people and animals emerged through her drawings and paintings. At age six, she produced an ink drawing of a seated cat, whiskers and tail curled around its feet. Even her landscapes smiled; trees assumed human shape, flowers lifted their faces to the sun. Her pictures illustrated scripture: "You will go out in joy and be led forth in peace; the mountains and the hills will burst into song before you, and all the trees of the field will clap their hands." (Isa. 55:12) I believe that on the day of her funeral, the sudden movement of the trees was a reminder of her eternal creativity.

Claire and I shared the same sense of humor. When she was twelve, our family flew to New York State. I don't remember why we didn't drive, but the airport scene is bright and clear.

With me I carried a book of "bloopers" which Claire had also read. We sat together, knees locked, hands shaking as we turned the pages. "Bertha, a missionary from Africa, will speak tonight at Calvary Church. Come tonight and hear Bertha Belch all the way from Africa," we read, suppressing giggles. "Ladies, don't forget the rummage sale. It's a chance to get rid of those things not worth keeping around the house. Don't forget your husbands." The giggles ballooned into sputtering laughter. "Pot luck supper at 5 p.m. Prayer and medication to follow."

By this time Claire and I were laughing so hard that no sound emerged; eyes flooded and overflowed; our stomachs hurt.

Bill and our other children stared sharply at us; then, embarrassed, all three walked away, pretending we were strangers. I still see them gazing out the airport window, ignoring us as they watched planes take off and land.

Two days before her death, Claire phoned me. "Do you remember that day in the airport reading bloopers?" she asked. We laughed all over again, recalling some of them to each other.

Knowing the intensity of the constant pain Claire suffered, watching her over the years as it increased even though she saw different kinds of doctors and visited pain clinics, it is still a miracle to me how her sense of humor and her deep faith enfolded her to the end of her life.

The pain began in her back, and then spread to her rib cage and chest. Over the years she had nerve blocks, rib surgery, and ever increasing pain medication. She continued to work, but finally applied for disability.

As Claire's pain increased, we found ways to overcome it through humor. Norman Cousins' book, *Anatomy of an Illness,* describes Cousins' recovery due to laughter, but it was Dave Barry, not Norman Cousins, who walked into my life one day when I saw his book, *"A Short History of the United States."* Reading it, I knew it was a Claire book and I bought one for her. We read portions to each other over the phone and laughed.

For two years after Claire's death I couldn't read Barry's column in the newspaper. Instead of humor, I felt pain. But now, once again, I can chuckle at his sense of humor and remember the mutual giggles with a sense of, if not joy, pleasure.

It wasn't just what Claire read or heard that caused the humor to spill over. Her childhood escapades were sources of practical jokes even when her life was in turmoil and stress her daily companion. Her niece Ivy, Wayne's daughter, tells of a time that illustrates this well. Claire was sharing with Ivy, then in her early teens, an event that Ivy says was "just too gory to try to picture." But as her mother, I knew it was typical of Claire's early years.

Ivy says, "Some friends of hers dared each other to tie a marshmallow on a string and stick it down their throats, then pull it back up. Of course Claire agreed to try this stunt. She got it down while gagging, but the other girls had to help her pull it back out. Finally a bloody marshmallow emerged and fortunately she did not choke to death. I told Claire that story freaked me out and she just laughed. Since I was staying for dinner that night, Claire announced that dessert would be served first. There on fancy plates were marshmallows attached to a string!"

Our family called various things "a Claire story" or "a Claire joke." We all knew what that meant.

It wasn't just the family who benefited from Claire's sense of humor. Her friend Laurie writes, "Claire and I found each other out of necessity. I was her sons' babysitter. By the time they grew up, I had become part of the family. Claire taught me to laugh. I was always too serious as a child and a teenager. She found humor in situations that would have sent me hiding under a rock. Chronic pain challenged and eventually crippled Claire's body but it never touched her heart. I realize now that it was her faith in God that allowed her to laugh and rest a little easier. She lives on in my heart, which isn't quite as heavy as it used to be."

Claire's life encompassed humorous deeds, creativity in art and writing, and compassion for others who were "underdogs" for one reason or another. However, her poor choices and sensitivity played havoc with her life.

CHAPTER EIGHT

Days of Grace & Mercy

Lesley and Claire

CHAPTER EIGHT

Days of Grace & Mercy

Claire was a child of the sixties; her artistic nature fit well with the culture of the sixties and seventies. She wasn't a sixties "flower child," but she sketched flowers whose blossoms appeared human. She and her roommate Roberta attended a three-year school encompassing all manner of art: painting, ink-drawing, history, portrait restoration. Claire's talent for cartooning and children's illustration emerged early during her studies.

Our first visit to the girls' damp, crowded apartment was an eye-opener for Bill and me. Strings of colored glass beads hung from the doorframes; a pet rabbit hopped about and crouched on the sofa like a cat. Both girls were working on a sculptured bust of each other. After Claire's death Roberta asked for the bust Claire had crafted, and of course we were glad to give it to her.

Protests, editorials, and music focused on the Vietnam War. Lesley married a man who had served in the Pentagon, and six months after their wedding, Claire called to say she was engaged to a veteran of the war. We had met him only once and didn't feel comfortable about this. The uneasy feeling that mothers sometimes have wouldn't leave me alone. "Why not wait six months," I said, "and make sure this is right?"

It wasn't just an uneasy feeling. I also felt this couple had nothing in common. Here was a man very sports-oriented, a salesman, and one without the sensitivity of our daughter. Claire was a complicated person with many creative gifts and compassion for others. She seemed unaware of the stark differences I noted. I told myself that some of these differences could be gender-related.

Later, like many other families, we would discover the terrible consequences that the Vietnam War had on our son-in-law. Many veterans of this abominable war suffered mental instability; others became substance abusers and still others homeless. Agent Orange had damaged some veterans as well. Claire's husband refused to seek help or join a support group even though his war experiences were unspeakable. Instead, alcohol became the palliative, as it did for many veterans of Vietnam. Flashbacks contributed to his abusive behavior.

Later, years after the wedding, Claire told me, "Mother, there was nothing you and Dad could do. I wasn't ready to marry, and it wasn't right. But I made the decision and I had to live with it."

Soon after this wedding, Bill and I began our time of spiritual searching. We prayed for direction and guidance in our lives. It was early in the seventies, before the Roe v. Wade decision for abortion-on-demand and I was still working in television. One night I dreamed of walking down a long hall with sick and dying people on either side. It resembled a Mother Teresa-like hospice. As I looked from one suffering person to another I cried out, "O Lord, there are so many! How can I help these people?" At that moment a door opened at the end of the hall and a nurse stepped out holding a blanketed baby, which she held out to me. "Here," she said, "this one is yours."

This one was indeed mine, and I began working with others in the pro-life movement, appearing on television, writing, and counseling, speaking at schools, churches, and civic groups. It was during this time that Claire's first baby died. The following year she became pregnant again, and the nursery door, which had been tightly shut, was reopened.

The night of April 3, 1974, a year after Roe, I was invited by Randolph-Macon Woman's College to debate the administrator of a large abortion facility in Washington, D. C. At break time I was called aside and informed that my pregnant daughter was in labor in the hospital, seriously ill, packed in ice due to a high fever.

How I ever returned to continue the debate I don't know; God's grace sustained me. And my anger spurred me on, thinking of the babies who were dying by one doctor's hand while another was trying to save a "wanted" premature baby.

The next two weeks seem timeless, without sequence. And yet as I look back, they followed a pattern of grief and distress so profound I don't know how our family survived it, except that the very hand of God rested upon us.

Our daughter lived, but our tiny grandson did not. I see a window splashed with sunlight and the anguished face of the baby's father and his words: "Tell me he will live!" The scene shifts to the nursery: Bill and I are gowned in white, a nurse is handing the black-haired infant to us for baptism; Bill takes water from a bowl held by the nurse and baptizes him. A few hours later, Matthew, our grandson, dies.

Hollow-eyed, our daughter joined the family at a graveside service with a tiny white casket set before us. As we stood there, a friend of mine caught something in her hand—something that had floated through the air. "Look," she said to me. As she opened her hand, I saw a pink rose petal.

A week later, Claire entered the hospital with a life-threatening fever and kidney infection. Our prayer groups and our pro-life friends prayed fervently for her. Like the Apostle Paul, I cried out, "Please do not give me sorrow upon sorrow!" (Phil. 2:27)

As death and the shadow of death surrounded us, I could pray with Job, "How I long for the months gone by, for the days when God watched over me, when his lamp shone upon my head and by his light I walked through the darkness!" (29:23) How abandoned I felt as grief and loss struck me down, and groaning continued in the core of my being.

"When we experience a loss, a hole opens up inside of us," writes Rabbi David Wolpe. "It is almost as if the loss itself plows right through us. We bleed through that opening, and sometimes old wounds are reopened. Things we thought were safely inside, patched over, healed, prove painful in the wake of the new pain."[6]

We did feel held up by the love of our friends whose tears and prayers encompassed us in the darkness and sorrow.

Sorrow turned to joy a year later when Claire delivered Jason, a healthy baby boy. But the shadow of sorrow fell across our paths, for three weeks before Jason's birth, Lesley delivered a premature baby girl, Christine, who would wear a body cast for eighteen months due to genetic abnormalities.

Throughout my life we continued to suffer loss and trials, yet it is not a platitude to say that God's presence, his grace, and his guidance walked us through each new difficulty. God showed me that as I spoke and counseled on pro-life topics, my life could be a testimony. An unwed pregnancy in our family as well as deaths of babies, and so-called birth defects all strengthened my ability to empathize with other women's fears and pain, and point them to the One who sees us through.

After Jason's birth, I suspected Claire's marriage was in trouble. She loved and cared for her active baby boy, she continued her artwork, and she visited her neighbors; but the death of two babies and marital conflict were obviously causing discord. She lived an hour away, and I remember driving up to the house with its drapes and blinds shut tight; the house itself appeared depressed, morose, unhappy.

Then Claire became pregnant again. In her seventh month, a kidney infection again threatened her and the baby. Fearful of another loss, I prayed fervently. Since the Holy Spirit had opened up the scriptures to us, I was not surprised when just upon awakening one morning, an angel appeared by my bedside. I didn't see his face, but the white robe shone with unbelievable light. It was a momentary appearance as a voice said, "Don't be afraid, Marilyn. He's a four-pounder." Now fully awake I pondered his words. What did "four-pounder" mean? When Chris was born, full-term, he weighed nine pounds. It must be that at seven months' gestation, he was already at a weight that would have seen him through a premature birth.

I found this angelic appearance both comforting and puzzling. But this experience was clarified when I read about the research A. Irene Strommen did in the Bible. She writes, "In the gospel of Luke alone I counted twenty-three references to angels, and thirty-two in the Book of Acts. I noticed that most of the writers of scripture had seen angels, heard God speak or peered into the invisible kingdom by means of a vision. As I read, I became sharply aware of the prominence given this supernatural dimension in Scripture, in contrast to its muted emphasis in contemporary Christianity."[7]

Although I haven't seen an angel since that time years ago, I have learned more about God's sovereignty in his relationship with us individually. Scripture admonishes us not to seek a sign (Matt. 2:38-39) but we find that God intervenes, providing signs or visions according to his will, as he did with Cornelius, Peter, and Paul in the Book of Acts. God is God: he can certainly answer our request for a sign, but it is more likely he will do so at a time of his own choosing.

When Jason was three and Chris only one, Claire left her husband and fled to our home in Lynchburg. Bill, Wayne, and I parked a truck at her door and packed hurriedly, taking the boys' furniture and belongings and a portion of the housewares, anxious to leave, fearing that confrontation with our son-in-law might lead to violence.

It was many years later before I knew the extent of her abuse and terror. We were sitting on her deck, a home we had purchased for her, sipping iced tea and listening to leaves stroke the railing. As she calmly related those terrible experiences to me, my visualization of the attacks choked me with tears and anger.

"I thought marriage was forever, and I had no right to leave," she told me. "But God knows why I had to go."

Some time after Claire left her home, I received a letter from her next-door neighbor, a lovely, intelligent Jewish girl, a non-believer. I had met her often over the years when I visited; at one point I gave her Francis Schaeffer's book *The God Who Is There*.

Jo Ellen wrote:

> I am sitting here with tears streaming down my face from missing Claire so much and not daring to compound her pain by telling her. And so it is to you I write to tell you of my love for your daughter.
>
> The scientist in me always searches for an explanation for things and so I have tried to analyze what it is about

Claire that makes me feel as I do about her. For I have lived in many places and said goodbye to many close friends and never felt so lonely as I do now without her. What is perhaps even more in need of an explanation is that Mark feels much the same way.

To begin with, in this day of women's liberation, so many women are demanding equal pay, equal opportunity, and freedom from responsibility so that they can pursue their all-important careers. Yet the most talented and creative person I know has readily and cheerfully put it all aside to devote herself to her family, with the security that she will pick it up later. As she daily tried to rescue Jason from one peril after the next, often operating on little sleep because she had worked until 3 a.m. and maybe held a sick Christopher till 5 or 6, there was never a sense of martyrdom. I hope you won't think me facetious when I say there was almost a religious nobility about her.

The poppies she painted in my kitchen which appear to be dancing to the breeze are a daily reminder of her cheerfulness. Mark will miss her waving to him each morning from the bottom of the hill as he finally manages to start his motorcycle.

We shared our families—both births and deaths—and I was always impressed with her wisdom and sense of humanity. She is the nicest and kindest person I have ever met. I can't put it better than Mark when he says, "Without her next door all our lives are the poorer."

I thank you for your letter to me, particularly now that it has made me comfortable enough to write this to you.

Love, Jo Ellen

CHAPTER NINE

Mother's Day

Gazebo on the grounds of Virginia Baptist Hospital

CHAPTER NINE

Mother's Day

I enter an antique shop soon after Claire's death. I hear my own intake of breath as I see the tall figure of a woman dressed in Victorian clothes, her full, dark hair touching the ruffle of her collar. The shape of her face and body, her blue eyes, the curve of her smile—how could it be—Claire?

Then in an instant I see her for what she is, a mannequin, stationary and stately, a bouquet of flowers positioned in her immovable hands.

Now tears form in my eyes. I want to hold my daughter once again in my arms, feeling her warmth, careful not to hold her too tightly and increase her pain. I remember holding her artist's hands with beautifully shaped nails, stroking her dark brown hair. I want to look into the china blue eyes and see her love as well as her pain.

Gerald Sittser describes the feeling I had and the feelings of others who have suffered the loss of a loved one. "I have photographs of Lynda, Diana Jane, and my mother on the mantel in our living room. I still have not gotten used to seeing them there. I gaze at photographs of people I once knew, and enjoyed, lived with, talked to, and held in my arms. Their pictures fall far short of what they were in real life and what real life was like for them. Immobile but lifeless, they are beautiful but dead, mere snapshots of people whom I knew as living people in the motion of our life together. They are poor replacements of the multi-dimensional relationships I had with them."[8]

Unlike me, Claire was left with no pictures of her first two babies that died. After she and her boys settled in Lynchburg, she was still grieving over the previous deaths. That's when she found The Compassionate Friends, a national organization designed to support grieving families. She attended meetings, sharing her thoughts with others who had lost babies and older children. "I read the obituaries," she told me, "and pray for each family who has lost a baby."

A few weeks after Claire's death, Bill and I attended that same support group. About thirty people sat in a circle, a combination of old and young men and women, some newly grieving as we were, others who had lost children years ago. I look back at that night in shame, for unaware that we were still in shock, we were almost proud, even arrogant, that we were living above the pain, wondering why others were so mournful. "We don't need to come back here," we told each other. "This can't teach us anything." How little we knew! We had not yet experienced any holidays or anniversaries since the death of our daughter. I had not yet lived through what is the worst day for me, Mother's Day.

Rooted in my childhood, memories of Mother's Day bring forth thoughts of sitting with my mother in church: she is wearing a white carnation, indicating that her mother has died. I am wearing a pink one, symbolic of life. At that time and in that place, mothers were praised and cherished in church services and in homes. Our florist business flourished on Mother's Day with orders of bouquets, corsages, plants, and flowers prepared for placement on graves.

Mother's Day was an important holiday for us as a family too. Claire, as well as Lesley and Wayne, had a close relationship with their grandmother. The essay Claire wrote, "His Perfect Love," showed her attachment to my mother and her respect for her.

When Claire was a working single mother, I frequently took her sons, Jason and Chris, to visit my parents in the nursing home. I grieved before their deaths, for my father, who died at ninety-four, and for my mother, who died at ninety. The grief came in gulps of sorrow and melancholia while I watched their decline.

They lived in an apartment after moving from New York to Virginia. They were with us in our four-generation household for several months. One by one they entered a nursing home. Missing my mother came during her lifetime as she changed from a gracious fun-loving person to a woman whose dementia prevented meaningful communication. I felt relief when she went to be with the

Lord. Still, when May rolled around that year, I looked longingly and tearfully at the beautiful Mother's Day cards that I had no need to buy.

Now I am a mother who has no mother and whose daughter has died. I no longer buy Claire cards and I no longer receive her little Mother's Day gifts. I have navy earrings, a star-shaped box, pressed-flower place mats, humorous handmade cards and drawings from her. On my last Mother's Day before her death, I received a note on her own design of "Thank You" paper, with ink drawings featuring mice (her illustrative trademark) and a drawing of herself as a little girl.

The note read: "Dear Mom, for all your acts of kindness, for all your loving words, for all your wisdom you graciously share and for being a wonderful friend to me beyond being a mom to me, how I love you!" After several years, pain and joy merge as I hold this paper. It is still hard to look at her handwriting.

It doesn't matter what age your child is when he or she dies or how long ago, the pain remains. That became clear to me several years ago when a woman came up to me at a church gathering with tears in her eyes. "My baby died at two months," she told me. When I asked how long ago that was, she said, "Ten years."

Early on after a death, overwhelming grief and stunning pain change the very motions of everyday life. Some people eat too much; others cannot eat at all. Sleep overcomes some and escapes others.

I developed a daily ritual that helped me cope. Since it was summertime and I lived close to a hospital whose well-kept grounds included a gazebo, I exercised in the fresh air by walking a mile, feeling warm breezes kiss my face, and absorbing the beauty of trees and bushes—crape myrtle and late blooming roses. I stopped at the gazebo and read the memorial plaque telling me of another child who had died at only three years of age.

I sat down on a bench in the gazebo to pray, to meditate, and often to read the Bible I brought with me. Hearing cars drive by and the tapping of feet on the pavement reminded me that life itself goes on, regardless of changes in my own life.

Though grief and tears are normal and necessary, the intensity of pain subsides in time. I felt comforted and changed. (Isa 61:3) God's comfort became a warm shawl, enveloping me and giving me strength, teaching me that death is a part of life, that we cannot know at the time how God will use these painful times to help others in distress. (2 Cor. 1:3-7)

A. Irene Strommen says, "I find it satisfying to think that God can work through events that seemingly make no sense, events he may not have wanted but that he uses to accomplish a future purpose."[9]

Pat Hylton, a woman in my church, came to that same conclusion and shares her own grief experience this way:

Losing a child must be the single most devastating and tragic thing that could ever happen to a parent and to a family. I thought this surely would be the end of me, the end of my sanity; I could not imagine how any one could ever get through such a terrible loss, until it happened to me.

The first days and weeks were like a fog or a dream. I think the Lord put me into a state of unawareness where I was able to function as if nothing terrible had happened. I was like this through the visitation and the funeral and for about a week after it happened.

Our son, Chris, had been a troubled young man, and struggled to stay on the right path through most of his teenage years. I remember almost immediately feeling a peace in my heart that he was with God; he was at peace. I could feel God pouring strength into me, helping me get through this terrible nightmare.

A year before we lost Chris we found out that he and his girlfriend were going to have a child. At that time I was so upset, asking the Lord why this was happening. He was so unready to be a father and accept the responsibilities of parenthood. I know now that this was part of God's plan. After Chris' death it suddenly became clear to me that in giving us his child, a precious part of him, to hold and pour our love into, allowed us to begin to heal. I felt like a part of myself had been torn from me, but that little baby helped fill in that empty space. "All things work together for good to them that love God." (Romans 8:28)

For a long while I could not watch the home movies of Chris, but after watching one and crying all the way through, I find now that it gives me a sense of peace and happiness to have those precious memories of him to share with his little girl.

It's been eight years since Chris' death and there is not a day that I don't think of him in so many ways. The tears still come, though not as frequently.

I have accepted Chris' death but I am still healing. It is something that stays with you forever. I would have been lost if God had not been with me every step of the way.

After the death of her first baby, Claire described a vision or a dream she experienced. In her spirit or her mind she saw a large square picture framing her in grief with scattered broken shapes surrounding her. Gradually, over time, the square became smaller, the picture less vivid and the shapes assembled themselves into a whole. "It's part of the healing process," she explained.

Sometimes we both knew we shared some kind of terror that no one else understood, and we tiptoed toward each other, but stopped, as if by acknowledging our shared fear, it would be real, and neither of us could bear it.

We overcame much of our fear through different kinds of prayer. After my trip to the Holy Land along with Bill and other believers, I stored a bottle of water from the Jordan River in my freezer. For several weeks I took a small amount to Claire; she and I dipped our fingers into the water, then held hands while we prayed. This too was a healing ritual, a quiet time together.

But all of our companionship did not center around ritual or prayer or pain. Besides Dave Barry, we shared other contemporary authors such as Elizabeth Berg and Reynolds Price, especially enjoying his book, *A Whole New Life.* We both liked the same television shows, particularly "Mama's Family" or "Dr. Quinn, Medicine Woman" (admiring Sully, her man). On nights when Bill traveled to prisons to teach, Claire and I had supper together, a special shrimp salad plate every time—our tradition—and after that we chatted, looked at her latest drawings, or watched a video. While we ate at her kitchen table with lighted candles and pretty place mats, Claire needed to get up, walk or stand intermittently due to her back, chest, and rib pain.

Claire's pain intensified while she was still working at Lynchburg Sheltered Industries as a program manager. She loved and encouraged her clients, disabled people, who worked in a controlled environment doing jobs tailored to their abilities. She taught classes on basic skills and hygiene, and sometimes went to court with them as their advocate.

Any movement increased her pain and affected her breathing. But she couldn't stay in one position very long, so no matter what she did, her pain was constant. Treatments by her osteopathic physician and nerve blocks by a neurosurgeon provided only temporary relief.

Due to allergies as well as physical problems requiring surgery, Claire took a variety of prescription drugs. I observed her increasing drug dependency, and her doctor tried to monitor her medications. Sometimes I was alarmed at her behaviors and moods. I knew she often forgot when she had taken her medications or how much. When I visited her during the last few months of her life, she occasionally seemed hallucinatory or semi-conscious, sleeping a great deal during the day. Yet none of us—family or physicians—seemed to know what to do.

Since Claire's death, much more has been discovered and documented about chronic pain and its treatment. Today perhaps there would have been a different kind of intervention and help.

As her mother, I suffered while watching her get in or out of a car, walk stiffly down the sidewalk, or even struggle to dress herself. Stress became my companion as well as hers. One day the evidence of my pain presented itself in a new form. Claire phoned me early one morning to tell me that working had become impossible and she was applying for disability. That's all I remember of that conversation, for my mind shut down and withdrew from reality. Bill told me afterward that I appeared in the bedroom sobbing, telling him about the conversation. I remember none of it. During a twenty-four hour period I had only brief episodes of conscious behavior. I have no memory of eating, dressing, or carrying on a conversation, although I was told I did all of these.

The next day I felt normal again, but had no recollection of the previous day except for those few snatches of time. My diagnosis was transient global amnesia, brought on by trauma or great stress.

After this episode, I reflected on the different ways our bodies and minds adapt to trauma. One of the results of my lost day was to help me identify with Alzheimer patients or those with other behaviors that they cannot control or remember. God showed me the truth of the passage in the first chapter of Second Corinthians. "God comforts us in all our troubles so that we may share his comfort and compassion with others."

CHAPTER TEN

His Sovereign Help

Claire, Jason, age 8, Chris, age 6

CHAPTER TEN

His Sovereign Help

Seeing the mannequin that looked like Claire was a startling moment, but there are strange, small things that cause a feeling of shock or, perhaps, emptiness.

"Suddenly here he is again," writes Nicholas Wolterstorff. "The chain of suggestion can begin almost anywhere: a phrase heard in a lecture, an unpainted board on a house, a lamp-pole, a stone. From such innocuous things my imagination winds its sure way to my wound. There's no forgetting."[10]

No, there's no forgetting, nor did I want to forget my daughter; I wanted to capture and contain the memories. My memories of Claire caused both comfort and pain, depending on circumstance. I could examine those memories, look at them, and then hide them in my subconscious. Or I could keep them out, leaving them free to be cherished, held, and wept over. I determined not to cover or bury them, but I found this hard to do. I wanted to rewrap them, hide them in a box, and tie the ribbons so the wounds that Wolterstorff mentioned would not be opened repeatedly.

How could I help myself to heal?

Some people attribute the saying, "God helps those who help themselves" to the Bible, but it is not found in scripture. However, scripture supports it. In reading the Word to find God's comfort for my grief, I observed the many ways we are encouraged to make an effort to help ourselves. I found directions to be still; to change, listen, meditate, and wait; to inquire and to sow; to both remember and forget. We are told to come near to God or to draw near to him and he will respond, he will come to us. "Seek the Lord, call upon him," says Isaiah.

Jesus gave instructions to those in need: "Stretch out your hand!" "Pick up your mat and walk!" "Wash in the pool!" The afflicted one is encouraged to be part of his own healing.

The third chapter of Colossians is revealing and helpful. By the power of the Spirit, I could let—allow—the peace of Christ to rule in my heart; I could let—allow—the word of Christ to dwell in me richly. I understood it was up to me to initiate these soul changes.

In reading an article by Anne Pach I found these six ways to help ourselves: "Be patient with yourself. Ask for and accept help. Accept your feelings. Lean into the pain. Look to your faith. Be good to yourself."[11]

By practicing every one of these six ways I began to heal. A few months after Claire's death, I decided to see a Christian counselor because I felt "stuck" in parts of my grief process. Counseling helped, and I could move on.

Through the years I have found that when I make a deliberate choice to help myself, God offers his sovereign help in unexpected ways. Some years ago after surgery for breast cancer, I experienced supernatural comfort and peace while lying on a hard table for many sessions of radiation. His word from the first chapter of Colossians penetrated my spirit just as the radiation penetrated my flesh. I had been reading these verses: "He is the image of the invisible God, the firstborn over all creation. For by him all things were created: things in heaven and on earth, visible and invisible, whether thrones or powers or rulers or authorities; all things were created by him and for him. He is before all things, and in him all things hold together." (15-17)

Early in my treatment, as a Star Trek-like machine directed its buzzing rays at the cancer site, I prayed my own words from these scriptures: "Jesus, Lord of the universe! You made all things! You made this invisible radiation! Heal me with your God-created energy."

Another day I prayed, "You who created all things, allow these rays to penetrate and heal."

At each time of treatment, the women who positioned me left the darkened room to enter the control room. One day I began my prayer and fell asleep!

By deciding to enjoy God, to worship him, to pray to him, I found him present in my trial, giving me his joy and bringing light into my situation by lifting me out of fear and darkness.

But God doesn't always say to us, First you must do this before I will do that. Through his unmerited love for us he may provide a sign of his presence unexpectedly.

For five months we lived in a four-generation household. My parents, our son and his wife and their baby all lived with us, producing intergenerational conflicts and personality clashes. Bill and I prayed for God's direction and his joy in our stressed-out lives. He showed us that loving confrontation (Eph. 4:15) would replace friction with peace and we found this guidance true.

One day, God's joy overtook me as I knelt on the floor with a basin of water washing my mother's feet while the baby lay kicking beside me. The indescribable presence of the Lord filled the room with sweetness and light. I don't recall what was said, but Mother and I burst into laughter and the baby joined in. That was almost thirty years ago but I still clearly remember that serendipitous moment.

I recall another day when God showed himself at a time of trial. While recovering from surgery in a large university hospital, I met a woman whose teenage son lay dying from an accident indirectly caused by his mother. As she sat by his wheelchair, her small body drawn tightly into a knot, I tried to make conversation. Finally she opened up and shared her story.

"My son loves the Lord," she told me, "and I've asked forgiveness from him and from God. Bobby can't hear me and often I feel God doesn't either. I feel so hopeless!"

"It wasn't your fault," I assured her. "And God does understand your suffering."

"I know in my head what you say is true," she nodded, "but my heart is so broken."

Two days later, my bag packed to go home, I met her in the hospital hallway. As we faced each other, sun streamed through a window, its reflection clearly forming a bright cross on the floor at our feet. Holding hands and watching this silent message from heaven, we sensed an inexpressible joy. His presence was so real that we embraced and wept.

Experiencing God's joy in our difficult circumstances is different from feeling happy. Happiness is transitory, earthly, and unpredictable. Amy Carmichael wrote, "Joy is not gush. Joy is not mere jolliness. Joy is perfect acquiescence—acceptance, rest—in God's will, whatever comes. And that is so, only for the soul that delights itself in God."[12]

There are no formulas to help us recover from grievous loss. We can try to help ourselves and fail; we can pray and still feel empty. But in the trying we find a God who cares for us; in reaching out we find he touches us. When we feel unnaturally depressed or unable to cope with our circumstance, that is the time to "ask for and accept help," whether it is from a counselor, a pastor, a close friend, or another family member.

It is a joy to discover later on how he met us in our time of trouble and in what ways he began to heal us.

Gerald Sittser tells us how the accident that took the lives of his three loved ones has changed his perception of God's sovereignty. He now believes that his former view was far too small. He says he believes God's sovereignty encompasses all of life, not simply tragic experiences but also our responses to them. God's sovereignty, says Sittser, transcends human freedom but does not nullify it.

Though I see through a glass darkly, I know Claire does not. She is in God's heavenly light, and I can rest in that assurance, knowing that God already knows when I will join her in eternal timelessness and praise. The missing of her will never stop until that time, but for me God's sovereignty has transcended my grief and lifted me into his marvelous light.

CHAPTER ELEVEN

Paul, Pain, & Humor

"Thorns" by Claire

Paul, Pain, & Humor

Claire used the Apostle Paul in her essay about pain showing both her sense of humor and her deep faith. She wrote:

"There was given me a thorn in my flesh, a messenger of Satan to torment me. Three times I pleaded with the Lord to take it away from me. But he said to me: My grace is sufficient for you, for my power is made perfect in weakness." (2 Cor. 12:7b-9a)

Obviously, Paul had a chronic pain problem. We can only speculate as to his specific affliction. Surely the pain was significant or Paul would not have pleaded with the Lord three times to remove it.

I, too, am afflicted with a long-term chronic pain syndrome, and I often ponder if God's grace is sufficient for me. Paul outwardly proclaimed: "Therefore I will boast all the more gladly about my weaknesses so that Christ's power may rest on me." (2 Cor. 12: 9b)

I cannot help but wonder what Paul really thought at times. When you consider his life, it could not have been easy to maintain his exuberance. I think about some basic and realistic differences between our sainted Paul and myself—although I, too, love the Lord with all my heart.

Pain has always been part of human existence, but Paul and I were born into different times, different cultures, and of course we have a gender difference. I, too, am single since my marriage ended many years ago. Unlike Paul, I have raised two children.

When my pain seems beyond endurance, the Lord touches me with a gift of humor. For instance, did Paul ever have to struggle into a pair of pantyhose each morning? It is a task beyond description with a thorn in one's side! No, Paul wore only a simple toga with an easy-tie sash. If underwear was necessary, I expect Paul wore easy pull-on boxer shorts.

And just how often did Paul have to lower himself into a bathtub, then call for help to get out? Did he bathe with any regularity anyway? He probably simply walked into the river with a huge bar of Lifebuoy™ on occasion. Big deal!

Apparently Paul chose not to marry and have a family so he could dedicate his life to spreading the gospel. In fact, he warned men of this distraction. Therefore, his "thorn" never bore the weight of a screaming child in the mall. Nor did he have to vacuum an entire house, sucking up Legos™ and miniature cars, sending shock waves into his thorn as they splintered in every direction and embedded themselves into walls. Let's face it— a dirt floor needs little care! Wet it down and ask an obese neighbor to stomp on it once a week!

I recognize that Paul walked more miles than any of us would consider reasonable—and without benefit of a pair of Reeboks™. But he also never had to car pool a load of hyperactive children to Skateland. Nor did he have to haul himself in and out of a sub-compact car that is more convenient than walking, yet holds you in its evil grasp as you attempt to get out with some dignity (underwear or not) without aggravating your thorn. A cart pulled by oxen is preferable but illegal on most highways today.

Since Paul did not marry and produce sons, did he have to drag trash cans to the curb each week? What did they do with their trash then? Give it all to the pigs? (Someone must know these things.) And what about lawn care? What with leaving home and living among dust and sand, Paul didn't have to worry. If he did, he could purchase a goat, or just say "To heck with what the neighbors think!"

With no electricity, Paul may have fashioned a heating pad out of non-flammable burlap and hot coals. Maybe the famous fig tree offered a soothing balm for pain. I would like to plant a fig tree and give it a try. (But could I dig a hole?)

And what about laundry? Since Paul wasn't married, did he simply stop a neighborhood woman or a disciple's wife and say, "Excuse me, but would you mind taking this load to the river? You see I have this thorn that prevents bending and banging clothes against the rocks." Of course, this was woman's work anyway!

Today we have conveniences that Paul never dreamed about. Rocks are now passé—at least in our country. Electric washing machines thoroughly clean and rinse our clothes. This leaves you with 100 pounds of wet, heavy clothing, which adheres firmly to the side of a metal drum. You need great strength in your back and arms as you bend over to disengage this incredible mess prior to heaving it into the electric dryer. This is a dreadful task for me with my thorn. Even bending and separating the wet load causes my thorn to protest.

And hey! Can you picture Paul on his hands and knees retrieving petrified food items such as furry green twinkies? I find it difficult to envision Paul stretched out under some kid's bed with a disgusted look on his face as he realizes that he is unable to get out of this ungraceful position (sans underwear—I still don't know this for sure).

I would like to talk to Paul. Get the real scoop. I would ask him about the sufficiency of God's grace for me too. Did each and every moment of his constant pain make him glad that God's power, perfection, and glory were proclaimed for all to see? Did he have moments of doubt or despair? Paul seemed to be zealous and clear on God's plan for him. I envy his certainty. Is God's power made perfect in MY pain? I do not know. Do I continue to persevere and endure? I must. God has been my trusted friend, Lord and Savior for so many years.

Yes, through the years God has carried me through personal tragedy (the loss of a daughter and a son), unspeakable physical harm, two near-death experiences and a journey of terror and fear. He was always there for me. Would he abandon me now? I know he will not. Will I know and understand his plan for me and this constant pain? I do not know. Trusting him completely is not easy. It is a day-to-day challenge. But I know without question that his love for me is certain and forever. I take comfort in this.

Perhaps, in unrecorded moments, Paul had similar thoughts. Maybe, after all, Paul could understand and relate to me. We may have more in common than I thought. Certainly our love for Jesus is a common bond. Paul may even have prayed as I do.

My heavenly Father,

Help me face a new day as it arrives. Replace dread with hope. One more day, bestow your measure of grace and let me live according to your plan for me. Help me to trust rather than fear. Help me to make you the priority rather than my pain. Help me to embrace the pain for your sake rather than despise it. Lovingly allow my tears and gently wipe them from my face. Forgive and embrace me in moments of despair. Allow others to see your face in my pain that they may come to know you.

"Surely I am coming soon," says the Lord.

"Amen, Come Lord Jesus." (Rev. 22:20 NIV)

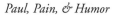
THORNS

"My grace is sufficient for you"
You told Paul
The thorn in his side would remain
Paul persevered despite your denial
I am valued no less by you
I dare not ask you again to remove my thorn
Yet I beg the same measure of grace
Precious Father, my life is yours
I deny myself gladly to be worthy
Surely, your grace is sufficient for me.
Your daughter,
Claire

CHAPTER TWELVE

Siblings—The Lonely Mourners

Lesley & Wayne
2003

CHAPTER TWELVE

Siblings—The Lonely Mourners

"Much has been written on the parental experience of losing a child but not as much attention has been focused on sibling loss," writes psychotherapist Elizabeth P. Welton, who lost an adult sibling. "Our grief is often viewed as less significant than the grief of our parents. It is not by chance that we are known as 'the lonely mourners.'"[13]

When a sibling dies, the bonds are fractured and the family history has a void that cannot be filled. I was unaware of this at first because, living my life as an only child, I could not imagine or understand the loss Claire's death was to her brother and sister. Perhaps I still can't.

Although our family suffered through many interactive trials, we remain close today. We've helped each other physically, emotionally, spiritually, and financially. Claire's brother and sister remembered her needs throughout her painful adult life.

Lesley and Dick opened their home to care for Claire's son, Jason, even though they had three daughters of their own. Jason lived with them for three years. While Claire was working at Lynchburg Sheltered Industries, suffering increasing pain and trying to raise two teenage boys, her sister offered to have Jason come live with them to ameliorate the stressful situation between the two brothers, and so reduce Claire's own stress and responsibilities.

Lesley says, "The fact that Claire let Jason come live with us speaks volumes of her love and concern for her sons. I think she knew at that time that this was the best thing for Jason, but how very difficult it must have been for her to let him come. From the time he came to us until her death several years later, I called her every Friday night and we would talk, laugh, and just generally enjoy one another. This is one of the things I miss the most, being able to talk to her on the phone. For a long time Friday nights seemed very strange and empty. But I am so thankful we spoke that Friday night before she died."

As adults, Claire and Wayne lived in the same neighborhood. Claire and her sister-in-law Diane would visit each other's homes, for as Diane says, "We had a lot in common from a shared wacky sense of humor to a strong creative drive. She was more a sister to me than a sister-in-law."

Since Diane was only three weeks older than Claire, they teased each other, and when Diane's fortieth birthday hit, Claire outdid herself. "I received black roses," says Diane, "black balloons and other gifts of doom, along with a special drawing, which now hangs in my office. Claire created a caricature of the two of us driving off in an overloaded convertible jalopy, her cats and my dogs hanging on for dear life as we ran away from home in a celebration of a mid-life crisis."

Because Claire owned two cats, her brother Wayne, who is allergic to cats, couldn't tolerate being in Claire's house very long. Wayne says, "My cat allergies drove me red-eyed and sniffing from her two-cat home. I always thought I hated cats but Claire insisted that I just never knew one well. Two months before Claire left us, all that changed. We were living in Texas then and a cat moved up the street and adopted us. For some reason, my cat allergies were now manageable and I quickly became attached to this animal just as Claire said I would. We sent Claire a photo of me holding the cat. She phoned us with a screech and howl. 'I don't believe it!' she yelled.

"I'm so glad she was still here to know I was a cat convert. To this day, every time I hold and stroke this cat, I am reminded of my sister, my playmate, my friend."

Wayne and Lesley cherish certain childhood memories too, sibling stuff that I never experienced.

"Claire was very good at creating something out of nothing," Wayne remembers. "When we were about six and ten, we sat on the floor of my closet to play games. Our favorite was playing 'Chipmunks.' Claire, the older, was the Head Chipmunk and I was her helper.

"As we grew older and our lives collided with the sixties, I decided I would like a wildly painted wall in my bedroom. Of course I turned to Claire, the artist and the sculptor in my family. With permission from Mom and Dad, Claire designed and then painted a mural in her little chipmunk's bedroom. After ten or twelve cans of spray paint and a ball of string and a full day, Claire unveiled her masterpiece, complete with the popular sixties icon, the peace symbol. I loved it!"

I had forgotten about that mural until Wayne told me about it, but recently I met Claire's former pastor who reminded me that she had painted a huge wall mural of children for their Sunday school room. "That was over twenty years ago," he said, "and just recently one of our members restored and updated it."

Lesley remembers that she and Claire, who shared a bedroom, would stuff a sock and throw it between their beds trying to hit each other. "We couldn't imagine why our parents were so unreasonable as to come up and threaten us with spankings if we didn't stop. We'd lie on our beds and giggle. Then there was the white spider that I would dream about. When I'd cry in the night, Claire would wake, come over and 'kill' the spider for me. I have a wonderful picture she drew of the two of us as kids with a spider on my shoulder."

Both girls played in their grandfather's greenhouses, using discarded flowers to play wedding or to arrange in rows on an overturned crate. They would run in the house smelling wonderful, stems and broken blossoms clinging to their hair while they paraded and giggled.

Some siblings don't have the good memories that our children do. When there's been jealousy or rancor, separation, or hateful actions toward one another, the death of a sibling causes different kinds of memories, regrets, and often remorse.

Just as Lesley and Dick opened their home to Jason, Claire opened hers to her niece, Ivy, when she was forced to leave her alcoholic and abusive husband, taking her five-month-old baby girl with her. Ivy says, "The fact that Claire would turn her life upside down for me and maybe even endanger herself made me realize what a caring person she was. She understood my situation since hers had been similar. Every morning she prayed and read her Bible before going to work, and she taught me how I could turn my life around through my relationship with Christ. Now, years later, I think of her when I have my daily devotional time, and I wish she could see my twelve-year-old daughter and meet my Christian husband and our little boy Benjamin."

Standing by the side of a brook one day, I found a stone in my pocket and I threw it into the water. As the stone hit the water, ripples fanned out in all directions, moving, moving, and causing the water to change its flow in an instant. Like the stone, my daughter's death hit me and I felt myself at the center of it all. Yet her death caused a ripple effect around me.

When we lose a loved one, we feel that grief belongs only to us and, caught up in our own pain, we are unaware that the life of the one we loved also impacted other lives, caused other people grief.

Besides flowers, food, and memorial gifts, Bill and I received over 300 cards of sympathy with precious words about our daughter.

"Claire was one of the few people I will ever know who I could talk to about anything," wrote a co-worker. "My life was richer because of her friendship."

Claire's former boss wrote us, "She was a beautiful, caring young lady whose faith and courage is an example for all of us."

The pastor who shared Communion with her when she could no longer attend church called her a beautiful lady who exuded the love of Christ and "bore her burden with more grace than anyone I knew."

And one older friend wrote, "If we were able to choose family, Claire would be part of ours."

About six months after Claire's death, the ARC (Association of Retarded Citizens) of Central Virginia honored her posthumously at their annual meeting. Her son, Chris, received the award on her behalf and the program read:

LIFETIME ACHIEVEMENT
Claire F. Kennedy

This award is given to Claire in honor of her many years of dedicated service to people with mental retardation and disabilities and their families. Claire was the first infant teacher for Project Daniel when the Association for Retarded Citizens started the grant project in 1978. Project Daniel was an early intervention program under the old LAARC School where Claire worked with special needs infants and their families. In 1980, Claire went to work for the Lynchburg Sheltered Workshop on Federal Street as a work activity teacher. She continued to serve people with disabilities in many roles as the Workshop moved to Odd Fellows Road and became a sheltered industry. Claire served as the adult basic education teacher and program manager there for twelve years, until her personal illness forced her into retirement.

A graduate of the Virginia Art Institute, Claire was a professional artist whose works depicting children and special needs were used in literature for many local and state displays.

Throughout her lifetime, Claire was an advocate for persons with mental retardation/disabilities. She cared for them and had a special gift, which allowed her to dedicate her life's work in this area. Claire was very active in her church and was a loving mother of her two sons, Jason and Chris. Claire F. Kennedy died on June 30, 1996, after a lengthy illness.

CHAPTER THIRTEEN

Losses & Promises

Ancestral Sampler
1791

CHAPTER THIRTEEN

Losses & Promises

An old sampler now hangs on the wall of our apartment. I found it folded in a box when my parents packed up for their move to Virginia. The 1791 sampler is the work of twelve-year-old Mary Hall (Polly). She was the first wife of my ancestor, Joshua Palmer. Born in Connecticut in 1778, Joshua moved to New York State and built a stagecoach inn on his extensive property. Historical records call him "the overseer of the poor." I envision him in knee britches, a well-to-do settler appointed by the local government to care for those in need.

Joshua suffered many losses typical of his day. Mary, who died early in life, is buried with her baby in nearby Greenlawn cemetery. Joshua's second wife, Abigail, also died, probably in childbirth. His third wife, Adeline Sanford, is my great-great grandmother, who lived to be ninety-six.

I think of Joshua's grief as he buried his wives and his infant children. And I remember my grandparents, Mary and Ernest, whose two children, my father's siblings, died in their twenties. Though suffering the unnatural pain of our children pre-deceasing us seems the worst possible loss, this suffering was even more frequent for our ancestors and for biblical people.

Men and women of the Bible are not cartoon-like figures to me, not flannel-graph dolls or video characters, but people of flesh and blood and bone whose bodies ached as they labored daily or traveled long distances by foot. Their eyes widened with joy, flashed with anger, or wept in sorrow. One of these women, Naomi, touches me deeply as I read her story in the Book of Ruth. I meditate on her strength and her deep love for her daughters-in-law, Orpah and Ruth, after all three women had lost their husbands. These women could not envision the complexity of our lives to-day—neither could my ancestor Joshua—but they shared our emotions, they formed relationships like ours, they worshiped our God.

Due to marriage, job transfers, or retirement, many of my friends and family have moved to new locations. Naomi and her husband Elimelech moved from Bethlehem in Judah to the land of Moab, due to famine. Then Naomi's husband died. Their sons, Mahlon and Chilion, married Moabite women; after several years these sons died too. Scripture does not tell us how or why. Naomi was then alone with no husband or sons.

News did travel in those days, even without phone, newspaper, or e-mail. Naomi heard that "the Lord has come to the aid of his people by providing food for them." (Ruth 1:6) So she planned to return.

I am moved by Naomi's compassion for her widowed daughters-in-law. Even though the two young women started out on the journey with her, she tried to persuade them to go back to their own family homes. Naomi must have loved these young women dearly. She kissed them. They all wept as she argued with them about going with her.

Naomi composed herself and jokingly asked them if she could have more sons, would they wait for them to grow up to marry them? Then, probably with sudden sobs, Naomi's grief and bitterness exploded as she told them "the Lord's hand has gone out against me!"

Ruth stayed with her ("Your people will be my people and your God my God," she told Naomi), and when they arrived in Bethlehem, Naomi was greeted by surprised women. "Can this be Naomi?" they asked. Like many today who call out angrily to God, "Why me?" Naomi told the women to call her Mara, which means "bitter."

"I went away full but the Lord has brought me back empty," she said, referring to her losses. Once again, she claimed that the Almighty had brought this misfortune upon her.

Now life took a turn for Naomi and Ruth, as well. By taking her mother-in-law's advice, Ruth did indeed find a caring husband,

Boaz. And this story ended joyfully for Naomi after her journey through a time of grief and bitterness.

Since Boaz was a relative of her husband, Naomi was blessed when Ruth delivered a son. The women, the ones who greeted her when she returned to Bethlehem, now called out to her, "Praise be to the Lord, who this day has not left you without a kinsman-redeemer. May he become famous throughout Israel! He will renew your life and sustain you in your old age. For your daughter-in-law, who loves you and is better to you than seven sons, has given him birth." (Ruth 4: 13, 15)

After suffering hardships and the death of loved ones, Naomi was blessed by God with the joy of a grandson, named Obed, who would become the grandfather of King David.

How I love the ending of Naomi's story as recorded in this book. I see this grandmother sitting quietly, her heart full of many emotions. "Then Naomi took the child, laid him in her lap and cared for him. The women living there said, 'Naomi has a son.'" (Ruth 4:16-17)

God worked out his sovereign purpose in the lives of Naomi, Ruth, and Boaz.

In his book *Trusting God*, Jerry Bridges writes, "The stories of Esther and Mordecai and Ruth and Boaz both had happy endings. We can see God's hand at work in those events. But what about the story that does not have a happy ending? Is God sovereign also?"[14] Bridges goes on to say that we honor God by choosing to trust him when we don't understand what he is doing or why he has allowed some adverse circumstances to occur. And that is what I saw in my daughter, Claire, throughout the trials of her life.

On one of her self-portraits, Claire inscribed these words from Jeremiah 29:11: "For I know the plans I have for you," declares the Lord, "plans to prosper you and not to harm you, plans to give you a hope and a future." These were words she treasured and held onto during her darkest hours. Although these words were delivered to the exiled people of Israel, Claire clung to this promise as a personal one.

After her death, I questioned God. How could she rely on his promise and not live to see it fulfilled? I know that a cloud of witnesses from Scripture and brave believers down through the ages have affirmed the sovereignty of God; that those who suffer on earth are in heaven now because they believed in Jesus, who suffered, died, and was raised for their sake.

The impact of Claire's faith and her works have affected so many lives for good that I see a purpose, though I cannot understand it. I must admit that reading this verse causes pain in my heart, and yet I accept God's sovereignty; I know my finite mind cannot grasp his eternal purpose.

His purpose for us as believers is to be with him. And so I shout "Hallelujah!" As I read from Revelation 22: "The throne of God and of the Lamb will be in the city, and his servants will serve him. They will see his face, and his name will be on their foreheads. There will be no more night. They will not need the light of a lamp or the light of the sun, for the Lord God will give them light. And they will reign forever and ever."

CHAPTER FOURTEEN

Blossoming

Claire's illustration

CHAPTER FOURTEEN

Blossoming

Most believers seek a closer walk with their heavenly Father, but don't want to pray "Do whatever you have to in order to bring me closer to you." Jerry Bridges writes "…we do not seek adversity just so we can develop a deeper relationship with God. Rather, God through adversity seeks us out. It is God who draws us more and more into a deeper relationship with him. If we are seeking him it is because he is seeking us,"[15] says Bridges.

Contrary to the axiom, time does not heal all wounds. Though time raised me from the depths of grief, only God's loving presence helped me to accept that my life would never be the same again. I remembered that resurrection follows crucifixion; that joy comes in the morning; that God's joy is not the same as earthly happiness. Only the presence of my loving heavenly Father allowed me to shout "Hallelujah!" and once again experience the spirit of praise.

I wallowed in a pond of grief for a while, even welcoming the darkness, adding my tears to the shadowy waters that engulfed me. But after a while, I looked up and out. I saw flowers growing on the bank of my pond; once again I perceived colors; memories of light and life pushed their way in. I knew then I had a choice to stay in the pond or to reach the bank, calling to God to pull me out.

"He lifted me out of the slimy pit, out of the mud and mire; he set my feet on a rock and gave me a firm place to stand. He put a new song in my mouth, a hymn of praise to our God." (Ps. 40:2)

I do not forget that I spent time in the pond. Because I was in there, struggling, I can help others who are now in that place. I assure them that by looking up and out, they will eventually climb out and once again find a measure of peace without forgetting where they've been.

"The healing process is one of slow repair," says Catherine M. Sanders PhD, whose sister died. "Success in grief work depends on accepting the loss and the changes that will have to take place in our lives. We need to absorb the idea that we will need to find substitutes and replacements but do not have to give up precious memories."[16]

Holding in regrets, remorse, or unforgiveness perpetuates grief. When I played tapes over and over in my head or listened to the voices that said, "I should have" or "Why didn't I?" the door to a renewed and vital life stayed shut.

One of the things troubling me after Claire's death could have been resolved beforehand, but Claire and I seldom talked about the death of her two babies and the circumstances surrounding them. The first baby had been stillborn. Her second, a premature son, died three days after birth. She looked forward to seeing them in heaven. But Claire's reference to "my little girl" reminded me that we had never named her. She had been cremated and we held a memorial service for her in the church chapel.

When I shared this painful memory with Margaret, my Christian counselor, she suggested that I hold a private ceremony and name the baby. At first I resisted the thought, but one day I knew I had to do something to heal this painful memory. If I didn't, I would play the tape over and over—"We should have"— and regret would settle in forever.

What should I do, Lord? I asked. As I prayed, I saw on my desk the wooden cross I had received as a child in Sunday school. I had often held it during prayer. Lighting a candle, I knelt, held my cross, and asked God to name the baby Emily Claire.

Relief from regret came quickly. I cried, pressing the cross to my heart, a little cross that had assisted many of my petitions. Sometimes I used an open Bible as I prayed. I think many of us who are evangelicals miss out on healing and reconciliation by refusing to accept practices which include the use of images or icons, not for worship, but for the sense of touch and sight that enhances our devotion to the Creator.

In his book *Satisfy Your Soul*, Dr. Bruce Demarest says, "Verbal prayer changes circumstances in the external world; contemplative prayer changes the inner world of the Christian who so prays."[17]

And I found an inner peace concerning this baby. No matter what fragment of grief still wounded me, I sought the Spirit's direction to help me heal.

For a time after Claire's death, reading scripture was a chore, but it was a discipline I knew I should follow. God's words were just that—words; they no longer filled me with joy or worship or even conviction. I could feel nothing as I read. But as time passed, God's Word to me had power again.

The verses that have strengthened me through life's trials are found in Philippians 4: 6 and 7. I have used the passage in contemplative prayer by savoring its individual parts:

Do not be anxious about anything
But in everything
by prayer and petition
with thanksgiving
present your requests to God.
And the peace of God
which transcends all understanding
will guard your hearts
and your minds in Christ Jesus.

When I ask, he answers. He gives his strength to me in my weakness, he counsels me and guides me, and he will show me his majesty and help me to understand his sovereignty, as much as I can with my finite mind and heart. To be nourished and enervated by his Word and Presence matures me in my faith for I need those things and energy daily.

This satisfies me for the time being, for this life. In another dimension, which I cannot see until I pass through the veil and join the cloud of witnesses, I will know joy that we never could imagine in this life.

I thought of the scripture read at Claire's funeral: "So it will be with the resurrection of the dead. The body that is sown is perishable; it is raised imperishable. It is sown in dishonor; it is raised in glory; it is sown in weakness; it is raised in power; it is sown a natural body, it is raised a spiritual body." (I Cor 15:42-44)

Two years after Claire's death, my cousin's husband, a church organist and a loving servant of the Lord, died suddenly in his sleep. Years before, Claire had served as flower girl in their wedding. Soon after his death, I dreamed of Claire, young, happy, dressed in black top and tights. She wore a crown of silver with sparkly moving objects. Wordlessly she smiled at me, dancing along a hall, holding a flower in her hand, opening doors as she went and waving her hands toward the openings. When I awoke, refreshed and energized from seeing her happiness, I realized she was showing me the many rooms that Jesus tells us about. But now in my earthly form, I could not see inside the rooms.

Some day, inside the rooms I will see what Jesus has prepared for me. A blossoming will come forth from death, a flowering of life eternal. Although I will daily experience the loss of my daughter, I choose to focus on memories of her and the sovereignty of God. I will join Claire and together with all of those who have gone before we'll worship the Lord in all his glory.

EPILOGUE

A Letter to My Daughter

Claire

A Letter to My Daughter

Dear Claire,

I'm sitting in church looking at the memorial flowers for the anniversary of your death. The early service is over, the church is empty. In the distance I hear the voices of people heading for Sunday school classes. Here, in the stillness of the sanctuary, I am remembering the day so long ago when you brought me a fistful of violets as a token of your love.

As a child and as a teenager, you were a free spirit, drawing, painting, playing your guitar, creating puppets and marionettes to delight the neighborhood children. But no, you weren't the perfect child. You could disappear, forgetting to leave a note. You never cleaned your room. You climbed a tree to hide while you smoked a cigarette, and once, on a dare, you risked your life walking the railroad trestle. But through it all, Jesus never let you go. You trusted him throughout your complex and painful adult life.

As I sit here now, gazing at the flowers, I'm thinking of you and the gift you were to your family and friends. I know you're still using your gifts in heaven, however God chooses.

I get up now and walk out the door, blinded for a moment by the June sunshine. A tall woman walks up to me. "The flowers are beautiful," she nods.

"Thank you," I say.

And I want to say thank you, my daughter. You taught me lessons about love and sacrifice and lessons about living with grace and dignity.

I'll be seeing you.

Love, Mom

END NOTES

Chapter One

1. (p. 6)   Wolterstorff, Nicholas. *Lament for a Son.* Grand Rapids, MI. William B. Eerdsman Publishing Company, 1987. p. 9.
2. (p. 6)   Arnold, Joan Hagan and Gemma, Penelope Buschman. *A Child Dies: A Portrait of Family Grief.* (Second Edition) Philadelphia. The Charles Press, 1994. p. 73.
3. (p. 7)   Sittser, Gerald. *A Grace Disguised: How the Soul Grows Through Loss.* Grand Rapids, MI. Zondervan Publishing House, 1996. p. 63.

Chapter Two

4. (p. 20)   Brokaw, Tom. *The Greatest Generation.* New York. Random House, 1998. From Book Jacket.

Chapter Six

5. (p. 47)   Strommen, Merton P. and Strommen, A. Irene. *Five Cries of Grief: One Family's Journey to Healing After the Tragic Death of a Son.* Minneapolis. Augsburg, 1996. p. 34.

Chapter Eight

6. (p. 59)   Wolpe, Rabbi David. *Making Loss Matter: Creating Meaning in Difficult Times.*
New York. Riverhead Books, a member of Penguin Putnam, Inc., 1999. P. 15.
7. (p. 61)   Strommen. p. 49.

Chapter Nine

8. (p. 65)   Sittser, Gerald. p. 82.
9. (p. 68)   Strommen. p. 79.

Chapter Ten

10. (p. 75) Wolterstorff. p. 98.
11. (p. 76) Pach, Anne. "Grief Along the Road." Newsletter, May 1997.
12. (p. 78) Carmichael, Amy. *"You Are My Hiding Place: A 40-Day Journey in the Company of Amy Carmichael."* Devotional Readings

arranged by David Hazard. Minneapolis. Bethany House, 1991. p. 76.

Chapter Twelve
13. (p. 89)   Welton, Elizabeth P. "We Need Not Walk Alone," The Compassionate Friends Newsletter, Fall 2001.

Chapter Thirteen
14. (p. 99)   Bridges, Jerry. *Trusting God.* Colorado Springs, CO. NavPress, 1988. p. 50.

Chapter Fourteen
15. (p. 103) ibid. p. 192.
16. (p. 104) Sanders, Catherine M., Ph.D. *Surviving Grief...And Learning to Live Again.* New York. John Wiley & Sons, Inc., 1992. p. 83.
17. (p. 104) Demarest, Dr. Bruce. *Satisfy Your Soul.* Colorado Springs, CO. NavPress, 1999. p. 170.

BIBLIOGRAPHY

Arnold, Joan Hagan and Gemma, Penelope Buschman. *A Child Dies: A Portrait of Family Grief.* (Second Edition) Philadelphia. The Charles Press, 1994.

Barry, Dave. A Short History of the United States (Dave Barry Slept Here: A Sort of History of the United States). New York. Random House, 1989.

Bridges, Jerry. *Trusting God.* Colorado Springs, CO, NavPress, 1988.

Brokaw, Tom. *The Greatest Generation.* New York. Random House, 1998. From Book Jacket.

Carmichael, Amy. *"You Are My Hiding Place: A 40-Day Journey in the Company of Amy Carmichael." Devotional Readings arranged by David Hazard.* Minneapolis. Bethany House, 1991.

Cousins, Norman. *Anatomy of an Illness.* New York. Norton, 1979.

Demarest, Dr. Bruce. *Satisfy Your Soul.* Colorado Springs, CO. NavPress, 1999.

Pach, Anne. "Grief Along the Road." Newsletter, May 1997.

Price, Reynolds. *A Whole New Life.* New York. Atheneum, 1994.

Sanders, Catherine M., Ph.D. *Surviving Grief...And Learning to Live Again.* New York. John Wiley & Sons, Inc., 1992.

Schaeffer, Francis. *The God Who Is There.* Downers Grove, IL. InterVarsity, 1998.

Sittser, Gerald. *A Grace Disguised: How the Soul Grows Through Loss.* Grand Rapids, MI. Zondervan Publishing House, 1996.

Strommen, Merton P. and Strommen, A. Irene. *Five Cries of Grief: One Family's Journey to Healing After the Tragic Death of a Son.* Minneapolis. Augsburg, 1996.

Welton, Elizabeth P. "We Need Not Walk Alone," The Compassionate Friends Newsletter, Fall 2001.

Wolpe, Rabbi David. *Making Loss Matter: Creating Meaning in Difficult Times.* New York. Riverhead Books, a member of Penguin Putnam, Inc., 1999.

Wolterstorff, Nicholas. *Lament for a Son.* Grand Rapids, MI. William B. Eerdsman Publishing Company, 1987.

To obtain additional copies of
Our Flower Girl:
A Story of Grief and Healing,
send the order form below to:
Marilyn Fanning
2100 Weeping Willow Drive, Apt. E
Lynchburg, VA 24501

- -

Please send:

_____copies of *Our Flower Girl* @ $12.00 each _____

Postage/Handling:

   $2.00 per book (first two books)   _____

   $1.00 for each additional book   _____

Total Enclosed (check only)   _____

Date_____

Name_____

Address _____

City_____State_____Zip _____